UNDERSTANDING STREET GANGS

By
Robert K. Jackson
and
Wesley D. McBride

D1057081

COPPERHOUSE PUBLISHING COMPANY
901-5 Tahoe Blvd.
Incline Village, Nevada 89451
(702) 833-3131

Your Partner in Education
with
"QUALITY BOOKS AT FAIR PRICES"

Understanding
Street Gangs

Library of Congress Catalog Number 84-71475
ISBN 0-942728-17-3 Paper Text Edition

6 7 8 9 10

Printed in the United States of America.

DEDICATION

Understanding Street Gangs, is dedicated to those peace officers, sociologists, public officials, criminologists, and students who are trying to understand the street-gang phenomenon, and are trying to ameliorate the violence and social disruption associated with it.

Robert K. Jackson
Wesley D. McBride

ACKNOWLEDGMENTS

The authors gratefully acknowledge the following entities for the assistance they provided us in our initial research of material for this work.

Los Angeles County Sheriff's Department

Los Angeles Police Department

Los Angeles County District Attorney's Office

California Gang Investigator's Association

California Department of Justice.

California Youth Authority

New York Police Department

Albuquerque Police Department

Chicago Police Department

Los Angeles County Probation Department

TABLE OF CONTENTS
PART ONE: THE PROBLEM

PART II: POSSIBLE SOLUTIONS

PREFACE

Understanding Street Gangs, is a pioneer work in a relatively new field of criminology and sociology. The text attempts to answer such qestions as:

Why do street (and prison) gangs exist?
What are the causative factors?
What is the impact of the street gang phenomenon on society?
How serious and wide-spread is the problem?
What can and should law enforcement, the criminal justice system, sociologists, and the public be doing about the problem?

Understanding Street Gangs was written by two veteran law enforcement officers with a combined experience of over twenty years assigned to specialized gang units. Both are respected authorities on the subject who have lectured extensively on the topic and have qualified as experts in court. Both hold advance degrees from recognized universities. Bob Jackson is a detective sergeant with a large modern metropolitan police department. Sergeant Wes McBride is a street gang specialist assigned to the youth services bureau of a large and progressive sheriff's department.

Understanding Street Gangs offers a thorough and detailed "plain-talk" examination of street and prison gang structure and activity in this country. The book includes information as to the genesis, structure, and philosophy of different types of gangs. Gang behavior, graffiti, violence, and secrets are exposed in this highly readable text.

Understanding Street Gangs fills the information gap found in most sociological literature on the subject. The text discusses gangs and their activity from a perspective generally not previously explored. The authors' view is from the realistic perspective of those who deal with the problem on a daily basis and at the "street level."

The text is divided into two distinctive parts. Part I, provides a detailed discussion of (1) the genesis and history of all major gangs, (2) factors which lead to the nurturing and growth of street gangs in a community, and (3) the typical organizational structure, hierachy, and philosophy of identified street and prison gangs.

Part II, focuses on the role of law enforcement and other segments of the criminal justice system in dealing with gang violence and other illegal activities. Several chapters are addressed specifically to law enforcement. They provide (1) guidelines for police specialization and gang unit management, (2) specialized patrol procedures relating to gang contact and control, (3) specific investigative techniques, and (4) elements of effective prosecution of crimes unique to gang activity.

PART I:
THE PROBLEM

PART I:
THE PROBLEM

INTRODUCTION TO PART I

GANGS MAKE MARTYRS OF LOSERS

By Sidney J. Harris

One of the homespun wits of the last century made the memorable observation, "You never see a gang rushing across town to do a good deed." Gangs, almost by definition, are fractious, unruly, or downright criminal. Most of all, they do collectively what few of them would dare to do individually. Mobocracy is the heroism of cowards.

A recent study of delinquents in the state of Wisconsin disclosed that most violent crimes of youth were committed by groups of three or more. The level of every gang, big or small, is the level of its lowest, least law-abiding member.

Parents of such offenders, when they are brought into court, invariably declare that their boys were "led astray" by the others, that they got into "bad company," though they themselves were not vicious. This sounds like a parental cop-out, but in a certain sense it is largely true. Normally, it takes only one bold and inflammatory leader to arouse the latent malevolence within the others; it is mischief, as much as misery, that loves company.

Gang members tend to be chronic losers, who can accomplish nothing individually, or who live in so depressed an environment that only by banding together can they exercise any influence over their lives. In both cases, they are as much to be pitied as condemned.

Frustrated persons form attachments to such gangs (by whatever name they may be called) precisely for this reason—they permit the worser part of themselves to dominate the better part by making their members feel heroic rather than guilty. Like the lads led sullenly into court, they show no remorse because they feel none. Becoming a martyr is the only way they can triumph over feeling a failure.

From *Strictly Personal* by Sydney J. Harris, nationally syndicated columnist. Copyright by and reprinted with permission of News America Syndicate.

THE PROBLEM: AN OVERVIEW

Gangs are now spreading through our society like a violent plague. Daily, countless news stories depict the tragedy of gang violence. The following excerpts document only the tip of the problem.

Item. . . . "A gang fight at a crowded park resulted in a seven year old girl being shot in the head, while picnicking with her family."

Item. . . . "Shot gun blasts from a passing car, intended for a rival gang member, strike a child on a tricycle.

Item. . . . "A shoot-out between rival gangs claimed the life of a high school track star as he jogged around the school track."

Police files throughout the country are filled with similar, equally tragic examples. Once gang attacks were rare; now they appear almost commonplace. At one time gang members used chains, knives and an occasional "zip gun" in their forays. Now they use shotguns, automatic rifles, handguns, and explosives. At one time victims of gang violence were predominantly rival gang members. Now, with the use of firearms, innocent bystanders are often killed or injured by stray bullets. Once gang violence was limited to minority communities and lower socio-economic areas, but now it has spread to many communities.

AUTHORS' PURPOSE

The purpose of this book is to share some of the authors' experiences with, and observation of, gangs and gang members. Much of the material presents general information of value to all readers interested in learning about gang activity. In Part I, the text places special emphasis on (1) the history and development of major gangs, (2) factors which encourage gang growth, and (3) the typical structure and philosophy of gangs.

Part II focuses on the role of law enforcement in dealing with gang violence. These latter chapters present (1) guidelines for police specialization and gang unit management, (2) patrol procedures (relating to gang member contacts), (3) investigative techniques, and (4) elements of gang prosecution. The authors' objective is to offer a combination of general information about gangs, as well as presenting law enforcement strategies that will be useful to police agencies and others who are interested in the street gang problem.

It would be naive to assume that there is any one solution to the gang problem. What is needed is a multifaceted approach. No one would be so presumptuous as to claim to have all the answers to the problem, but the writers' extensive day-to-day exposure to gang members has allowed them to see major deficiencies in our current systems. By correcting some of these deficiencies, there could be a great reduction in the problem of gang-related violence that is currently being experienced

CHAPTER 1

THEORETICAL CONSIDERATIONS

HIERARCHY OF NEEDS

Why do gangs exist? There is no simple answer. For every sociologist that has studied gangs there seems to be a different theory. Dr. Abraham H. Maslow established his "Hierarchy of Needs" theory which states the various needs that must be satisfied before an individual can attain some level of happiness and satisfaction with his lot. Dr. Maslow postulated that the most basic human need is that of survival. He then built on that basic foundation five levels of human need leading to the ultimate level of self-actualization.

The following chart shows the different levels an individual must progress through in order to achieve self-actualization.

I.	**Physiological:**	Eat, Sleep, Body Needs
II.	**Security:**	Work, Save for Future
III.	**Social:**	Join in Clubs
IV.	**Self-Esteem:**	Display Talents and Skills Desire for Recognition
V.	**Self-Actualization:**	Self-Starter

Dr. Maslow then states that for an individual to proceed from one level to the next, it is not necessary for the preceding level to be completely satisfied. It is sufficient that only some level of satisfaction be obtained, and this level would, of course, change with the individual.

Level I

Dr. Maslow's theory can effectively explain the behavior of street gangs. The development of a street gang member according to Dr. Maslow's theory, for instance, begins at Levels I and II and is related to the manner in which the gang member seeks to satisfy these basic survival needs (e.g., food, water, etc.). A child learns early how these basic needs are to be met. If he observes his parents committing illegal acts to meet their needs, then he will pattern his behavior after theirs. If he is not corrected, the establishment of a mindset that lends itself to antisocial behavior and later a gang mentality will more than likely develop.

Level II

Once an individual has obtained a measure of satisfaction at Level I, he will then, according to Dr. Maslow, proceed to the second level: security. Here, the individual seeks to assure himself that his survival is secure for both the present and the future. For the future gang member, as for others, this need is met through his belonging to a family unit, weak as it may be.

Level III

When the maturing human has deviated from established norms in his acquisition of Levels I and II and has established his anti-social behavior patterns in satisfying these needs, he is ready to proceed to the next level—the satisfaction of the need to belong. It is at this level that gang membership is first seen.

The individual will begin to socialize with others who have also learned to use socially unacceptable means to satisfy their primary needs for survival and security. This socialization may result in further criminal activities as groups form and orient themselves around burglary or theft, narcotics dealing or drug abuse. In its most serious form the group will evolve into a violence-oriented street gang.

This grouping of peers was referred to as "Play Groups" or "Street Corner Groups" by early social scientists. It was, for all intents and purposes, a method that children gravitated toward in an attempt to fill unconsciously their need for socialization, or Maslow's Level III. These earlier researchers felt that play groups or street corner groups degenerated into gangs when their activities became delinquent and began to conflict with the established society's norms or with other groups in their areas.

A lack of parental guidance, not surprisingly, often contributes to the formation of a youth gang. The lack of love and respect from the family, along with the deterioration of the family unit, drives the young person elsewhere to satisfy his need to belong. Other gang members understand his need and supply an abundance of camaraderie, respect, and even a form of love.

This process does not take place overnight, of course, but involves a slow assimilation of the youth into the gang. Older members have been informally observing the development of the recruit and gradually allow him to associate with the gang. Once he reaches an age where he can prove himself with peer leaders within the gang structure, he may perform some sort of rite of passage or ceremony which officially recognizes his full membership. This process is called "jumping in." Alternatively, he may be simply accepted into the gang and does not have to prove himself in any particular way.

Level IV

After a period of time, the new gang member, who now has satisfied his need for companionship, begins to flex his muscles and strives to improve his position in the gang. He is, thus, progressing to Maslow's Level IV: the desire for recognition of skills, talents, etc. In Hispanic street gangs, where a member's *machismo* (manhood) is constantly being tested, self-esteem and recognition are extremely important.

The ego of the gang youth must be inflated to an extreme degree. In many cases the youth will have minimal financial or worldly assets; therefore, his most important possession becomes his reputation. A "hard look" or minor insult directed at a gang member by a member of a rival gang must be avenged, for such "hard looks" threaten not only his own self-esteem but his standing within the gang, and by extension, his identity. It is this attitude that results in the blood baths often seen on Los Angeles streets. A gang member seldom forgets or forgives a rival gang's intrusion on his "space"—whether it is his personal honor or his neighborhood.

Level V

The young gang member strives for superiority in all aspects of gang life. He will, on the surface, exude an air of easy self-confidence and a disdain for the non-gang community. The authors have interviewed several thousand gang members over the last ten years and have found this attitude to be a front intended to bring adulation and fame. However, this bravado is often quickly dropped when the individual is away from his fellow gang members or out of his neighborhood. For him, though, the adulation of fellow gang members is the attainment of self-actualization or Level V, distorted as it is from Maslow's initial concept.

CAUSATIVE FACTORS

Aside from the above factors, gangs exist because of a myriad of other social and economic factors. The combined elements may be pictured as a wheel, with each causative factor a spoke in that wheel. The more spokes, the stronger the wheel; the fewer spokes, the weaker the wheel. The prospective gang member's family unit forms the hub of this wheel and supports the whole. While the body of the gang, itself forms the wheel's rim. This cohesive unit binds together a force that once set in motion is most difficult to stop.

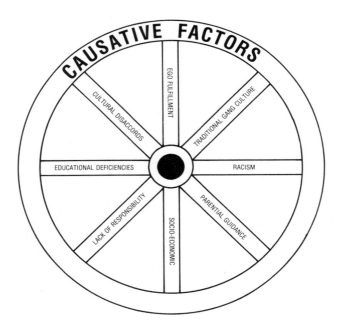

Figure 1.1 Why street gangs exist—causitive factors.

Keeping in mind that all of the causative factors (spokes) illustrated need not be present (nor are all possible factors necessarily shown) to form the atmosphere necessary for the breeding of a gang member, let us examine a few of the more important factors in the formation of prospective gang members.

RACISM

Racism obviously played an early and important role in the formation of street gangs in California. A study of existing gangs revealed that few are racially mixed. Black gangs are totally black. Mexican gangs allow few black or white individuals to join, but some Mexican gangs do have a sprinkling of black and white members. Usually these individuals are culturally Hispanic. They were born in predominantly Mexican-American neighborhoods and their formative years were spent in these communities. In probation camps the black and white youths who associate with Mexican-American gang members are called "want-a-be's" by their peers, referring to their desire to be Mexican. On the other hand, white gangs are traditionally white only and tend toward a white racist philosophy.

SOCIO-ECONOMIC PRESSURES

The native Mexican immigrating to California in the early part of

Figure 1.2 A community perspective.

the twentieth century was looked upon by the Caucasian population as a source of unskilled, cheap labor. This attitude, along with the political racist views, relegated Mexicans to *barrios* (i.e.,neighborhoods) comprised of an almost totally Hispanic population. This situation was reinforced by a continuous flow of immigrants who preferred to live where their native language was spoken and customs practiced.

It was not long before competition for jobs between the growing immigrant population and native Californians led to hatred and rivalries between the groups. These rivalries grew to neighborhood vs. neighborhood disputes as more and more Hispanics were packed into the *barrios,* and this demographic distribution led directly to the formation of today's Hispanic street gangs. The same set of circumstances, with only minor deviations, led to the formation of street gangs of African and Asian ancestry.

FAMILY STRUCTURES AND PROFILES

Another, and probably the most important causative factor in the formation of the gang member, is the family structure. It is primarily the family atmosphere that will influence the direction to be taken by the youth in the future. The authors have found certain common threads running through most families having hard-core gang members.

Figure 1.3 A typical Hispanic neighborhood mural.

Prevalent Factors

The family is quite often, but not exclusively, a racial minority and receives some form of government assistance. In addition, the family often lacks a male authority figure. A typical profile of a gang member's family unit could be illustrated as follows: a single mother, mid-thirties, with three to four children, living in a common-law state with a male who very likely does not exercise positive disciplinary action over the children. This male figure may be a criminal or drug addict, and therefore represents a negative role model. The family income is less than the average reported in the United States Census of 1980 for an East Los Angeles *barrio* resident (i.e., $7,000 per year). Typically neither adult has more than an elementary school education. The children live with minimal adult supervision and tend to associate with other youngsters who come from similar homes.

Profile of Matriarchal Family

Female off-spring often become unmarried mothers before they are eighteen. When one of the children encounters law enforcement authorities, the dominant figure (usually the mother) makes excuses for the child. These excuses normally take the form of accusations against society in general. Thus, children are taught early that they are not responsible for their actions and are shown how to transfer blame to "society." By the time the youngsters reach their mid-teens, they have become accustomed to blaming society for their problems. They truly believe that they are victims and that they have the absolute right, if not the duty, to do whatever they want, whenever they want.

Family With Gang Lineage

A second type of family profile that is very common, and many times nearly indistinguishable from the first, is one that may have two strong family leaders in a mother and a father. In these cases, the parents are usually graduates from gangs themselves and see little wrong with their children belonging to gangs. In fact, such parents often encourage their children to belong. This type of structure is conducive to what is known as an assembly-line production of gang members. Law enforcement investigators and community social workers are thwarted at every turn by these families and have little, if any, success in influencing members away from their gang. Instances are also known in which one or both of the parents actually have participated in planning, and in some cases implementing, raids on rival gangs.

Family of Hispanic Cultural Background

A third family profile that commonly appears, is one in which the parents are non-English speaking and their customs are from a Hispanic cultural background. The children tend to adapt rapidly to the American way of life and enroute lose respect for their parents and the "old ways." These youths, who are generally English speaking, quickly become experts at manipulating their parents who lose all control over them.

The parents are generally law abiding, upstanding citizens who labor each day to make enough income to provide the basic necessities for their family. They are proud and tend to try to handle family problems themselves. When a member does eventually come up against the legal system, the family is dismayed by the lack of fortitude demonstrated by a fragmented, inconsistent and unresponsive juvenile justice system. Feeling abandoned by an inefficient legal system, this family meanders through life losing out to the gangs that are seducing their children.

Family With an Atypical Member

The fourth easily recognized family profile is that in which the parents strive to raise their offspring to be productive members of society. For unknown reasons, one or more of the children become uncontrollable, hard-core gang members while the remainder do not. These families usually try to "straighten out" the gang member, but once he has become hard-core there is little it can do.

Overlapping Family Profiles

Four basic family profiles have been discussed from which gang members regularly come. This does not, however, imply that these four are the only profiles that occur—only that they are the most common. These overlap, and often it is difficult to find a single, clear-cut example of one family type which does not share some elements with other family profiles outlined above.

LACK OF PUNISHMENT

Some gang members have stated that the lack of punishment for their actions when arrested has led to their continued gang activity. In a 1977 article on the California Youth Authority (CYA), the *Los Angeles Times* reported that the average time spent in jail by CYA inmates for murder and manslaughter was only 26.3 months.

The gang member, in his own unique way, is very conservative. He is a firm believer in capital punishment or life imprisonment for capital offenses. The authors have been told innumerable times by gang members after the murder of a fellow gang member, "We'll take care of it ourselves." When questioned as to why the gang does not assist the police to make an arrest or aid in prosecution, the standard answer is, "We've seen your system."

The gang member may be uneducated, but he is not without intelligence. He realizes that the chances of a convicted gang member being severely punished are minimal; and until society can convince them that justice will be fairly administered, the gangs will see no alternative but to continue to avenge their own.

The typical gang member is "street smart", able to fend for himself, and accomplished in the art of manipulation. He sees the lady of justice not only as blind, but as somewhat foolish; and, therefore, a likely target for manipulation. Thus when he is brought before the bar of justice, the gang member reverts to his survival mode, playing upon the sympathies of "soft" juvenile justice and an apathetic juvenile correction system. Offenders realize that serious offenses are not likely to be dealt with severely until repeated offenses have been tabulated

THE OUTLOOK

Arrests and time spent in probation camps build a member's gang status, establishing little or no incentive for him to break the cycle. Nor do the disciplinary programs that youth offenders are exposed to provide any adequate alternate role models that are effective in counteracting the allure of gang membership. It will only be through strong and adequate alternate role and life models that the youthful gang member will be persuaded to change his lifestyle. Until then, weaning the youth away from his gang will be unlikely.

ANOMIE

If a gang member is exposed to a social class and a level of affluence well out of his reach—with no explanation or in-depth counselling on socially accepted methods for his legitimately attaining a similar level —he will very probably turn to crime to satisfy his desires. Melton calls this transition from legitimate to illegitimate means of obtaining success, "anomie" or "a state of normlessness."

It is thought that given proper counselling and educational opportunities designed to reinforce socially constructive behavior, the gang member will have less cause to fall into a state of normlessness and will have more incentive to strive for legitimate, socially acceptable means for achieving satisfaction. Gang members respond to responsibilities. The few social programs that have demonstrated marked success were those that placed responsibility on the individual. Many gang members have slowly drifted away from the gang life when given a job requiring the demonstration of responsible behavior in return for a constant wage. Once the gang member sees the fruits of his labor (e.g., pay raises, promotions, acceptance and trust of co-workers and employers) he has a clear choice as to the direction his life will take.

Figure 1.4 A typical Hispanic neighborhood park.

ASPECTS OF GANG MEMBERSHIP

Now let us look at the positive and negative aspects of gang membership, from the perspective of the gang member. Imagine a scale, the scales of justice if you will. By placing all of the advantages of gang membership on one side, and all of the disadvantages on the other (remembering that these are being looked at from the viewpoint of the gang member), it is obvious that there are greater advantages in belonging to a gang than not (*See Figure 1.5*).

After a hard-core gang member has reached his late teens in the justice system, he is very likely past social redemption. He must make the decision himself whether to continue with his criminal career, or make the effort to "go straight." His lack of education and job skills often make it unlikely that he will choose to leave the gang where his talents are respected. For example, a lack of self-discipline and a violent temper are unacceptable traits in the non-gang society, but in the gang system he can turn these "liabilities" to his advantage by letting go completely and building a reputation as a *vato loco* ("crazy guy").

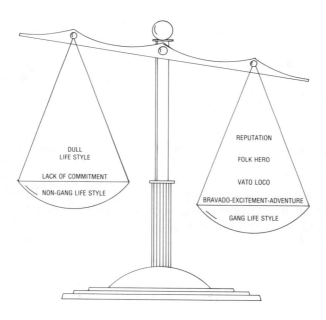

Figure 1.5 Depicts advantages and disadvantages of gang membership.

Similarly, the gang member knows that if he is killed by a rival gang during a fight, he will be viewed as a fallen hero by his home boys. His name will appear for years to come painted in gang graffiti throughout the *barrio*, and his exploits will be told and told again until reality is forgotten and a legend created.

Incarceration or injury build a gang member's status in the gang. This status guarantees his continued involvement with the gang as he tries to surpass his own reputation. Each time he returns from jail or the hospital, he has a bigger reputation and more scars to boast about. Impressionable youth who are toying with gang membership, view him with awe and begin to emulate him, thereby assuring the gang of future members. Thus what would ordinarily be viewed as character defects anywhere else, are admired by gang members. Values in this way are turned upside down; making that which is bad, seem good.

Once the gang member has attained the hard-core *vato loco* status, he is thoroughly a part of the gang culture, and sees no future for himself outside of his membership. He has learned his skills well and knows he can satisfy his need for acceptance and respect with violence, and with little likelihood of serious punishment.

Figure 1.6   Hispanic neighborhood business district.

PREVENTION

Prevention, when possible, is the best way of keeping gangs from forming in the first place; and logically, it is reasonable to assume that if a significant number of youth are deterred from entering a gang, future problems would be greatly reduced.

Counselling Programs

Currently there are numerous family, drug counselling, remedial education programs, etc. in existence in gang impacted communities. Unfortunately, many of these programs are so fragmented as to be almost useless. More emphasis must be placed on helping the family unit. Those programs that encourage family unity and involvement must be utilized to their utmost. These programs may involve anything from family outings to child abuse prevention. If the family is salvaged as a whole, and humanistic behavior patterns are established early in a youth's formative years, there will be less likelihood of his needing a gang to fill a void in his life.

Sports Programs

Similarly, sports programs for youths should also be strengthened. A young person involved in sports generally has greater self-respect and is less likely to seek reassurance from other gang members.

Educational Programs

As stated earlier, education is of the utmost importance, but one of the most difficult programs to enforce. To convince a young person who is not sophisticated enough to see beyond tomorrow, that he must prepare for the future, can be an exercise in futility. For instance, although programs in birth control, abortion, venereal disease prevention, etc., are common, one seldom sees any long-range programs (such as life planning) offered. Economically deprived youths must be counselled to see the importance of education in improving their future. Realistic programs must be developed to show young people that they can pull themselves out of poverty by setting attainable goals and then striving toward those goals.

Through education, the youths can be exposed to worlds they never dreamed existed. Gang members are often conditioned not to see beyond the boundaries of their neighborhood, but education can show that there are alternatives. They can be shown the value of obtaining skills that guarantee a place in a productive society.

Work Experience

Industry, which relies on the ghetto and *barrio* youth for laborers, must also be shown the potential value of training youth and in exposing them to leadership and management programs. Through involvement in community development, businesses will assure themselves of a dependable labor force for the future.

It would be idealistic to state that family unity, educational opportunities, and job training programs would be successful in all, or even most, of the cases. However, if these were applied in a consistent, constructive manner, we believe that many border-line youths would choose to forego the "advantages" of gang membership. Once exposed to a varied job market and to the benefits of a sound education, a youth with a stable family background will be more likely to become a productive and law-abiding member of society. But what must be done when all preventive programs fail and the youth goes on to become a hard-core gang member?

Need For Punishment

A repeated violent offender who will not respond to programs or opportunities offered by the courts and law enforcement, must be removed from the community so that he cannot continue to influence the other young people around him. This kind of offender must be housed in a penal facility away from impressionable youth teetering on the verge of becoming gang members.

The gang suppression units of the Los Angeles Police Department and Los Angeles County Sheriff's Department have both observed that when the small but central core of a gang's leaders are incarcerated, the activity of the gang is greatly reduced. The gang tends to remain in a sort of suspended animation, absorbing abuse from rivals and awaiting the return of the *vato locos* to lead it against its enemies.

It is this small informal group of influential members that must be separated from the main group. If their negative influence can be removed permanently or for long periods of time, the leaderless peripheral members are vulnerable and more likely to respond to the types of programs outlined earlier.

CHAPTER 2

GANGS DEFINED AND PERSPECTIVES OF GANG ACTIVITY

"GANG" DEFINED

Defining what a gang is would appear to be relatively easy. However, there are many definitions as to what constitutes a gang, each definition reflecting its own perspective. Paraphrased, Webster's *Dictionary* defines a gang as a group of people associated together in some way; specifically, an organized group of criminals, or a group of children or youths from the same neighborhood banded together for social reasons. Although this definition is accurate, it is too general to be practical. Block and Niederhoffer view gang behavior as a universal and normal adolescent striving for adult status, while Thrasher says that a gang does not become a gang until it begins to "excite disapproval and opposition." Cohen, on the other hand, defines a gang as a subculture with a value system different from the dominant ones found in the inclusive American culture. It is a collection of working class youth pursuing their delinquent activities in consort with one another.

Miller, in 1975, may have offered the most complete definition, when he explained that a gang is a group of recurrently associating individuals with identifiable leadership and internal organization, identifying with or claiming control over territory in the community, and engaging either individually or collectively in violent or other forms of illegal behavior.

One of the simplest and most functional definitions for this work is: *A gang is a group of people that form an allegiance for a common purpose, and engage in unlawful or criminal activity.*

WHAT IS GANG ACTIVITY?

Gang activity is a complex term to define. Its meaning is as varied as the background and perspectives of those attempting to define it. It is neither practical nor necessary to try to examine everything a gang does. In fact, many gang activities are shared by a large portion of society. But when a gang is involved in a weekend party, a fund-raising car wash, or even a family picnic, the potential for violence and criminal activity is far greater than for any other group of people. Unquestionably gangs pose a serious threat to society because of this inherent violence that is associated with their activities. A tragic example of this type of gang violence recently occurred in a Los Angeles area park. The park was crowded with families. Members of a local gang were also there. Rival gang members drove by, and after an exchange of insults, a gang fight erupted. The clash ended as the rivals fled to their car, removed a gun and fired into the crowd, shooting a seven year old girl in the head.

Such tragic examples of totally innocent victims being injured or killed continually follow reports of gang activity. To offer a   single definition of gang activity is to oversimplify a complex problem. In order to understand the problem, various perspectives of gang activity will now be examined.

The Community's View of Gang Activity

If there could be an overall picture of gang activity shared by society it would be based on the community's exposure to gang activity. This exposure results from observations and direct contacts with gangs or gang members, or through press and news media coverage of gang incidents. Although the general community learns of gang activity from published accounts of the violence, some neighborhoods are continually terrorized by gang attacks. These gang attacks are often followed by acts of intimidation. Gang members threaten victims and witnesses if they report incidents to the authorities. The gang is able and willing to carry out these threats

Some law-abiding citizens are prisoners in their own homes, fearing to go out at night. The streets belong to the gang. School activities are

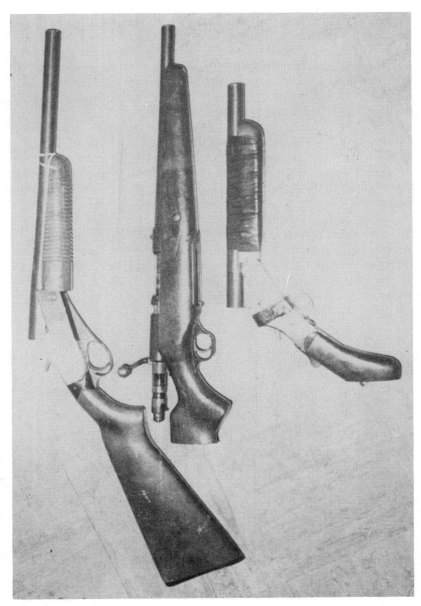

Figure 2.1 Typical gang weapons.

disrupted and innocent children are exposed to both planned and spontaneous gang attacks. Amusement parks in California, such as Disneyland, Knott's Berry Farm and Magic Mountain, as well as neighborhood parks and beaches where families go for fun and recreation, have erupted into battlegrounds for gangs. Victims range in age from infants to the elderly. A chance meeting at an amusement park between rival gangs all too often ends with innocent non-gang victims being seriously injured. This type of incident is not uncommon. Police files are filled with similar and tragic examples.

While gang violence makes headlines, gang members create even more damage on a regular basis to local property and businesses. Vandalism in the form of graffiti, and the wanton destruction of public and private property, serves to further a gang's reputation. Abandoned houses are a favorite target for vandalism, but even occupied homes do not escape. Local businesses suffer not only from property damage and graffiti, but from loss of customers and employees. Many customers avoid gang areas, while employees daily risk becoming victims of gang violence themselves. Businesses facing decreased revenue and rising insurance costs close their doors or are forced to move from the area. This cycle leaves another abandoned building for the gang. However, the majority of the residents of the affected area, because of

Figure 2.2 Mural with graffiti claiming area as street gang's "turf."

a profusion of social and economic factors, are not able to absorb their losses and move on. They will stay in the neighborhood, live in fear, and hope for an end to gang violence.

The News Media's View of Gang Activity

Most people ordinarily base their understanding of gang activity not on direct experience, but rather on news reports. Generally all violent crimes are reported by the news media in a similar fashion, regardless of the gang involvement.

There are two basic schools of thought when it comes to reporting gang violence. One group believes that naming the specific gangs responsible for the violence is beneficial. They believe that they are not releasing any confidential information that will hamper investigation or jeopardize society. After all, the gangs already seem to know who was involved without any assistance from the news media. Identifying these gangs serves to increase public pressure and to focus law enforcement attention toward the most violent gangs.

On the other hand, many newspeople and police officials are attempting to limit the individual gangs' public exposure. It has long been felt that identifying the specific gangs involved in a violent inci-

Figure 2.3 The streets belong to the gang!

dent tends to increase gang violence overall. Gang members are rewarded for their violence with press coverage. Publicity enhances the gang's image by spreading its reputation for violence. This is very important to the individual gang member, and many keep scrapbooks of newspaper clippings describing their gang's exploits. Rival gangs have been known to increase activities to get the recognition from the news media they feel they deserve. Regardless of the media's policy in reporting gang incidents, the violence continues to grow.

A precarious balance must be maintained between the reporting of a growing threat to society and sensationalism to increase circulation or boost the ratings. The task of reporting gang incidents objectively is further complicated because the problem is more prevalent in lower socio-economic areas. There comes a time when inner city gang violence no longer receives publicity—partly because it is no longer considered newsworthy due to the volume of crimes reported, and because its impact on the total community is limited. Yet when gang activity spreads to community areas where it is uncommon, or if the violence is particularly atrocious, then it is not only reported, but embellished.

The impact of the news media on the gang problem should not be

Figure 2.4 Prisoners of their environment?

directly measured by increases or decreases in gang violence, but by the overall exposure of the total problem. Special news reports and in-depth studies of gang activity and violence serve to increase the public's awareness. The public in turn adds pressure to the various governmental agencies and encourages that special attention be directed toward the problem of gang violence. Thus the relationship between gang activity and media coverage exists, but is difficult to prove conclusively.

The Gang's View of Gang Activity

A gang member views gang activity differently from the general public. Traditions of solidarity and neighborhood cohesiveness run deep. Pride in one's neighborhood, however poor it may be, is intense. The gang member has a driving need to belong and will often profess it in his last, dying breath. He not only needs to belong, but needs to tell others where he is from. This becomes so important that the greeting "Where are you from?" (or, in Latin areas, *"Deconde?"*) is the standard form of introduction on the street. Violence may follow a rival's response. Challenge a gang member's *barrio* or gang, and the challenger is challenging his total being. Further, he will proclaim the status of his *barrio* or gang as number one on almost any markable surface or wall. To a gang member, graffiti represents his pride in his neighborhood. It is a gang advertisement; it marks the territory or turf, and stands as a challenge to rivals (*See Figure 2.5*).

Figure 2.5 Graffiti proclaims the Dogtown Gang as number one.

Graffiti marking is not the member's only activity. "Partying" and "getting down with the home boys" is an integral part of gang life and offers members social contacts perhaps not previously available. Loyalty outweighs personal interests. An individual cannot merely assimilate into the gang without proving his toughness and worth to the group. He must see himself as a soldier protecting his turf in an ongoing war with rival gangs. He is expected to prove himself in battle. It is not uncommon for a gang member to seek out situations where he can build his reputation. Often these incidents follow a party or other gang function. When the member is accepted by the gang, he is expected to share with fellow members. This includes narcotics, alcohol and money. The gang is the first and most important part of his life.

One should keep in mind that most gang members are unskilled and poorly educated, especially during their younger, active years. The member's lifestyle options are limited to such an extent that criminal activity seems to be the only acceptable choice. These types of activities increase the gang's cohesiveness and perpetuate its identity. In turn, the gang offers the member protection, alibis and total acceptance.

The School's View of Gang Activity.

Gang activity in the schools mirrors that carried out in the adjacent community. Although most street gang members have always been of

Figure 2.6 School playground in street gang area.

school age, gang activity and violence on school campuses were uncommon in the past. That is not true today. Now we find many incidents where gang activity has disrupted the educational process and threatened the safety of students and teachers. As with other gang-related problems, the presence and seriousness of gang activity in the schools vary greatly depending on the school, the neighborhood, and the city. The problem begins in the elementary schools and grows to serious proportions in secondary schools. Schools are a good meeting place for gangs and often serve as a base for their activity.

Depending on the type of gang and the school atmosphere, the member may wear identifiable gang clothing and accessories. Various types of jackets, hats, scarfs or earrings are but a few of the items used. In the past these gang indicators were unnoticed or misinter-

Figure 2.7 School building in gang area.

preted by teachers and school administrators as being simply a new style of dress. Today, informed teachers report notebooks with graffiti-style writing appearing even at the elementary school level. This signals future problems, for once gang values become entrenched they are difficult to eradicate.

Gang activity on school campuses is evidenced by various symptoms. Acts of vandalism, arson and graffiti painting, although secretive in nature are often considered gang related. Stabbings and shootings between rival gangs take a toll of innocent students and teachers. Extortion of fellow students and intimidation of teachers also occur. The presence of a sufficient number of gang members in a class effectively renders the teacher powerless to enforce discipline or to teach. Teachers and administrators are threatened with beating or death if they report the criminal activity of gang members or testify against them in court.

School administrators are adopting a firm posture when dealing with gang disruptions and violence. To combat the violence specifically attributed to gangs, school security personnel are becoming gang experts. Security officers, trained in combating gang violence, saturate potentially violent situations to prevent gang confrontations. Yet even with this coordinated effort between school personnel and local police authorities the problem continues. All indications show that gang problems on campus are growing each year and spreading to areas previously untouched by gang violence.

Further complicating the situation are the programs for student opportunity transfers and a busing program that seeks to balance area schools racially. Beyond accomplishing the goals they were designed for, they serve to spread gang violence. It is hoped these programs will not be prolonged any longer than is necessary. When a gang member is moved from one school to another, whether singly as in the opportunity transfers, or as part of a group as in a busing program, violence follows and spills into community areas adjacent to the schools.

Law Enforcement's View of Gang Activity

Most law enforcement agencies regard gang activity as a study in violent crime. Gang violence and gang-related deaths continue to increase each year, taking a toll of innocent and non-gang victims. In order to combat this growing problem, law enforcement agencies direct much of their effort toward reducing gang violence. These efforts range from community awareness programs to selective enforcement units. Agencies working within budget confines must make the best use of their available resources. Manpower is limited and must be deployed to concentrate on the most violent types of criminal activity. The more violent gangs receive most of the law enforcment attention, and then only for the length of time that they are criminally active.

The reason for this attention by law enforcement is not merely because the group is a "gang," but rather because the gang is violent and criminally active. Gang violence is contagious and can rapidly spread throughout a community. Gang crimes are viewed by gang specialists as more dangerous than other crimes because they are not isolated acts, but links in a chain of events that must be broken.

It is generally agreed that all gangs cannot be eliminated, but their violent activity can be curtailed with continuing attention by law enforcement authorities. Realistic goals should reflect a coordinated effort among the various parts of the criminal justice system and the community.

CHAPTER 3

GANG STRUCTURE AND ORGANIZATION

HISTORICAL BACKGROUND

The gangs that initially developed in California included street gangs, car clubs, and prison gangs whose memberships were comprised predominantly of Hispanics, Caucasians and Asians. This California phenomenon has spread throughout the western United States to areas in Oregon, Arizona, Utah, Texas, New Mexico, Nevada and Colorado. Of special interest within this growth pattern are the Latin or Hispanic gangs, because of the similarity of their internal structure wherever they occur. In many cases, core members of Hispanic gangs, who had lived in California, returned to their hometowns in other states, and established their own gangs that imitate California street gangs in structure and activity.

HISPANIC STREET GANGS

The structure of Hispanic steet gangs is similar throughout the western states. Codes of conduct have been established from which traditions have evolved over generations. These traditions are not written, but handed down orally from generation to generation and are referred to as *Movidas* (*See Figure 3.1*).

Leadership

Leadership roles in Hispanic gangs are not formally recognized

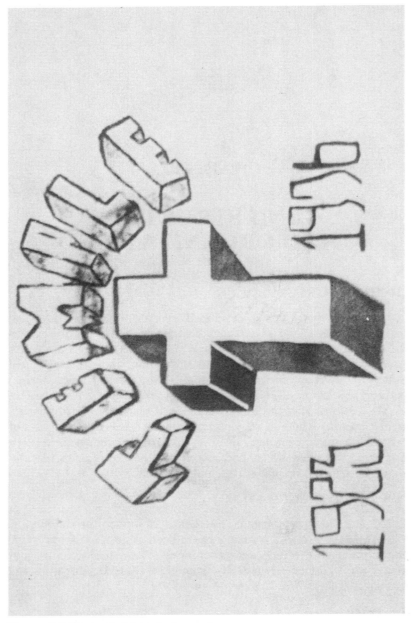

Figure 3.1 Hispanic historical gang logo.

positions. No one is elected to posts such as president, vice president or warlord, as they are in some eastern gangs. Leadership positions are not usually assumed by any one individual on a permanent basis, but by any member who has demonstrated unique qualities of leadership needed by a gang at a particular moment. Because of this loose structure and fluid leadership pattern, it is difficult to identify who the leader is at a particular time upon initial contact. Often, Hispanic gang leaders do not recognize themselves as leaders. For example, if a gang is attacked by a rival group, the victim gang looks to the most experienced fighter available at the moment within its own group, to coordinate the retaliation raid. This type of individual is referred to as a *vato loco* ("crazy guy"), and is generally a hard-core member with an extensive record of violent behavior. He will direct the retaliatory strike and then, having fulfilled his purpose steps aside, no longer being the leader. With small gangs, however, it is more likely that a single individual will be a recognized leader; though generally the more common pattern is not to have a fixed leader but a core of leaders—each with his own specialty—waiting to be called upon to lead the group as the situation dictates.

On the whole, these street gangs lack a solid infrastructure or chain of command and cannot operate efficiently as a total unit. Therefore, from necessity, they have divided themselves into groupings called "cliques."

Cliques

Cliques are normally formed according to age of the members. A clique will have its own name—Winos, Tiny Locos, Locos, and the like—and gang members may identify themselves by their gang and clique. On occasion, they may refer only to their clique membership. Although usually based on age, some cliques may be organized according to a specialty. There are gangs that have cliques that specialize in violence, and the majority of the "shooters" (gunmen) usually belong to that clique. But generally, each clique will have a number of individuals capable of violent behavior or responses. Once in a particular clique, newly accepted gang members remain in it throughout their gang careers. The clique may change or alter its name as it matures, but the same individuals tend to remain in close association with each other.

Nicknames

Most gang members adopt nicknames (monikers) when recruited into the group, if they do not already have one. The gang tends to be realistic in this respect, and will ordinarily select a name that fits the individual's physical or psychological characteristics. Nicknames are frequently chosen on the basis of some obvious characteristic the individual has, such as *Gordo* ("Fat") or *Flaco* ("Skinny").

Gang Names

The gangs themselves usually adopt names that have some geographical significance to their neighborhood: i.e., street names, hills, valleys, and occasionally old traditional neighborhood or regional names. Examples of this practice would be Maravilla (regional), 18th (street), Lomas (hills), or a combination such as Geraghty Loma (street and hill). The gang sees itself as the protector of its neighborhood from all aggressors, be they rival gangs or government agencies. To many gang members this so-called turf becomes their world. The locale outside the neighborhood becomes the unknown and is therefore dangerous. Inside the neighborhood the gang member considers his turf as a sanctuary, safe from the outside world. In some cases, gang members do not attend school because many of the schools are located outside their turf and they must pass through the turfs of rival gangs, which is dangerous to do. Gang wall writings (*placacios*) or graffiti are also an extension and identification of the gang and are used to identify the boundaries of its turf. Names, then, have great significance for Hispanic street gangs, for through the use of names, pecking orders, intra-gang relationships and home turf boundaries are given structure and definition. Once identified, the structure which the names give must not be scorned or changed.

Dress

The uniform or dress of Hispanic gangs is an easily recognized standard. Most gang members adopt a basic dress style: sparkling white T-shirts, thin belts, khaki pants with split cuffs, a black or blue knit cap (beanie) or a bandana tied around the forehead similar to a sweat - band. They refer to the bandana as a "moco" rag. There appears to be no meaning behind the colors worn by Mexican-American gang members as there is for the colors worn by Black gang members.

Loyalty To The Gang

A gang member is loyal to the death to his gang. He is proud, even boastful of his membership. If for some reason the Hispanic gang

Figure 3.2 Hazard Gang mural naming cliques within the gang.

Figure 3.3 Graffiti depicting nicknames: "Oso, Santo, Huero," and "Toby," of the 80th Street Gang.

member's family moves from his home gang's turf, he will not exchange loyalties with a gang in his new home. He will either fight them and return at every opportunity to his home gang's turf or make an alliance with them that allows him to maintain his identification with his home gang in his neighborhood, if there is no hard-core gang already established there. In this fashion, new gangs are established and developed.

Loyalty To The Code

A traditional gang member will never inform or turn *rata* ("rat") on his home boys, even if faced with death or prison. Loyalty is given at any price. A gang member will seldom disgrace himself or his family by turning informant. However, on rare occasions, weak gang members will turn on the gang. In addition, the gangs which are victims of other gangs will not testify against the rival gang, preferring to handle the retaliation themselves.

Female Gang Members

Female gang members, by contrast, have no inherent right in the gang, but are present only at the sufferance of their male counterparts. This sufferance is maintained, however, only insofar as the females conform to the mores of the youths. Equal rights and thoughts of equal rights for women play no part in Hispanic gangs. Females have their place within the gang structure and adhere strictly to that place. The female members are, by and large, separate cliques of the larger male gang. There are also very few female gangs that are totally separate entities.

Female members of male gangs are somewhat less restricted by the traditions that control the physical movement of males and can move among other gangs without the constant threat of death. This bizarre exception against the violation of territory of other gangs allows females to gather intelligence information for their own gang. And since all gangs benefit from the ploy, the maneuver is tolerated.

Figure 3.4 Female street gang members.

However, even though the ploy is allowed, the mere presence of females from an opposing gang often fans passions which frequently erupt into uncontrolled gang violence.

Conduct While in Prison

As previously stated, usually there are no written rules of conduct for street gang members. But the hard-core member is often a prime candidate for prison, and there are strict rules of conduct for Hispanics while incarcerated. These rules are called *movidas,* or inmate rules. They have been written down on occasion, but exist generally as oral repetitions of long-standing, traditional codes of conduct. The rules are similar from institution to institution and even carry over into the streets. The *movidas* are not necessarily restricted to gang members, but can apply to all Hispanic inmates. Many such rules exist to protect the fragile self-concept that Hispanic gang members frequently have of themselves; but most importantly, the rules assist the inmate to maintain his self-concept as a hetero-sexual male, as any intimation to the contrary not only implies homosexuality, but at the same time attacks the very integrity of the person not as a human being, but as a man. The rules or *movidas* maintain Hispanic *puro*—the "pureness" or integrity of the race.

The following excerpt from the *Youth Authority Quarterly* was written by Ramon Mendoza, an inmate of the California State Penitentiary. Mr. Mendoza, an admitted member of the Mexican Mafia, graphically describes the indoctrination process of new inmates in the prison system. His experiences are typical of those gang youths processed through the criminal system. The remarks are included here so that the reader can perceive these authentic experiences firsthand, from one who has actually lived them.

> In November of that year, I distinctly recall being in juvenile hall as a result of this arrest and seeking out an older inmate known as "Bugsy" for the purpose of having him explain to me the "movidas" or inmate "rules." Remembering me from Stevenson Junior High, he agreed.
>
> He related to me that Chicano inmates had to stick together at all times and that socializing with Black or White inmates was strictly prohibited. He told me that if any other inmate tried to push me around, I was supposed to react with violence immediately. He emphasized to me that even if I were to receive an ass-whipping, I would nonetheless prove that I was not a coward and would not tolerate verbal or physical taunts or challenges. He explained that it would be substantially more difficult for me because I was not a member of a street gang and, therefore, had no reliable credentials. Neither did I have any "home boys" (fellow gang members) to turn to for support. He told me that I should never show any weakness because by doing so I would leave myself vulnerable to other inmates and would become a "stoneout" or reject; Chicano inmates would not consider me a fellow Chicano, and the Black and White inmates wouldn't ac-

cept me either. In other words, I would be a nobody. This indoctrination session lasted for about a half hour and when "Bugsy " was finished, I shook his hand profusely and thanked him for spelling out the do's and dont's. He left quite a sobering impression on me and the words that kept flashing in my mind were: "Don't show weakness," "Stick with your race," "Respond immediately with violence," and, most important of all, "If you become a 'stone out', no one will recognize you." I was afraid of being a nobody.

Mr. Mendoza found that the rules were the same when he transferred to another institution. On this occasion he said:

So it was all about proving myself again. By this time, I had also heard stories of how inmates would look for a "pretty" inmate in order to turn him into a "punk" or "queen" (homosexual), and I learned that any homosexual advance by anyone, even in jest, was to be repelled immediately with violence. Chicano inmates were especially sensitive in this area. One of their exaggerated "movidas" (rules) required that if anyone touched a Chicano's behind he was to respond with violence. There were other rules such as not smoking after a black or white inmate and not bending over to pick up anything. The reasoning on the latter was that this was tantamount to giving a sexual invitation.

As humorous as this appears on the surface, the image was the reason for these rules. Indeed many Chicano inmates themselves would joke about the absurdity of most of their *movidas*. They would make remarks such as, "You better not slow down because I'm right behind you," or "If you bend over just one time, it's all over." But rules were rules and everyone understood the consequences of breaking them. It is interesting to note that the inmates adhered to their own rules much more enthusiastically and fervently than to the rules of the institution or, I might add, to the rules of society. Correspondingly, the gang code on the outside was followed and observed in a similar manner.

The *movidas* outside the institution were generally the same as the rules in camp with a few additional ones. The group structure in Paso Robles, for example, was set up by the inmates so that every cottage had its ethnic leaders. The Chicano group had a "Prez" (president), and a "Visa" (vice president) in each cottage. Each group had its own rules which had to be followed.

By way of conclusion, then, not all gangs, either in or out of prison, seem to have the same level of ethnic cohesiveness and identity as do the Hispanic gangs. Our attention now will be turned to other groups.

BLACK STREET GANGS

Black street gangs have existed in the Los Angeles area for many years. In the 1920's the Boozie gang was very active, committing street crimes around 18th Street and Central Avenue. A large family named Boozie was the source of most of the gang's members. During the late 1930's the Slauson gang was one of the most active. In the 1950's and 1960's additional gangs appeared with such names as the "Businessmen," "Home Street Gang," and the "117th Street Gang." These gangs went virtually unnoticed by the general public. Their lack of exposure was due to there being relatively few gangs and to the limited geographic range of their activity. They concentrated their criminal activity within the black neighborhoods. These early gangs have now faded out, and their members have been sent to prison or simply have grown old and died.

Presently, the number of black street gangs and their activity levels seem to follow varying cycles; at times almost non-existent, while at other times many gangs become active and violent. The most recent cycle began to emerge in the early 1970's.

At that time a group of young high-school age thugs began to terrorize their local campus and the neighborhoods in which they lived. This gang called themselves the "Crips" and extorted money from other students and were involved in violence. For instance, during one attack, a victim was held against a wall while a gang member carved "Crips" on his chest with a knife *(See Figure 3.5)*. With this example fresh in mind, it was not uncommon for a few of the members to approach another youth and ask him to join their gang. If his answer was no, he would be beaten senseless and left on the ground. Next day the gang would again approach the victim and repeat their offer. Each refusal to join resulted in some form of physical abuse.

Thus, four choices were left to the victim. He could join, flee, face repeated violence, or seek assistance. Unfortunately, school officials and the police were unable to provide continuous protection, and this led a number of the victims to form their own gang for protection against the Crips.

Most of these gangs tended to be made up of neighborhood groups, which in their own turn, followed in the street gang pattern of violence. This type of activity grew, and in a matter of a few years many neighborhoods had their own gangs. The violence of the groups was directed not only at rival gang members, but often at innocent non-gang victims. Thus the cycle fed itself.

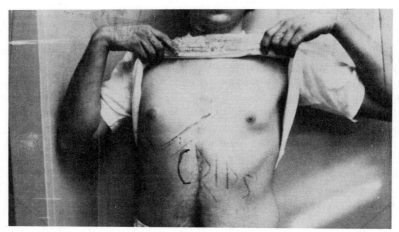

Figure 3.5 Victim of gang violence. Note "CRIPS" carved on victim's torso with a knife.

But in the mid-1970's an interesting change occurred. For a variety of reasons, the Crip gang built a strong reputation for being the strongest force in the black street gangs. Soon other gangs started renaming themselves, incorporating the word "Crip" into their new names. Gangs such as "Main Street" became the "Main Street Crips." Many others followed suit and soon gangs such as the "Kitchen Crips," "5-Deuce Crips," and "Rollin' 20's Crips" appeared. Although these gangs adopted the "Crip" name, they maintained the same leader and membership, and were independent—sharing only a common name.

Some of these rivals continued to fight among themselves, and a polarization of forces apparently had developed from these feuds. The black gangs divided themselves into Crips and non-Crips. In street or gang terminology, the factions were called "Bloods" (non-Crips) and "Cuzz" (Crips).

Black street gang activity is no longer an isolated problem. Clashes are no longer just between local neighborhood gangs, but have extended to include larger groups outside the neighborhood. Also, the local gangs have spread through California and into other western states. The activities of such groups, as is well known, are not restricted to gang feuds, but involve crimes of various sorts committed in affluent areas.

Finally, black street gangs differ significantly in many ways from Hispanic groups, as will be discussed below.

Traditional vs. Non-Traditional

Most Latin street gangs are considered traditional. That is, many of them have been around for two or more generations. Parents, and in some cases even grandparents, were members of the same gang. There is a sense of continuity, of family identity. Black street gangs usually have only a few veteran members, and the gang itself usually does not have a well-defined infrastructure. Moreover, the Black gang member is not as turf oriented and loyal as are Hispanic groups to their own areas. If a gang member moves to a new neighborhood or school, he will typically join the gang which exists in his new location. Black gang members, for whatever reason, tend to be more transient. Even in his loyalty to the gang, the black gang member is more oriented toward individuals within the gang rather than to the gang as a unit itself.

Other Conventions

The conventions regulating gang membership, modes of dress, and colors as identifying symbols are more flexible among black groups than not. Black gang members are more individualistic in this respect than are Hispanic, although some limited conformity is adhered to. Black gang members, for instance, will occasionally wear ear studs, hats or carry canes for identification, which contrasts markedly with the more traditional Hispanic *cholo* style of dress.

Furthermore, black gangs tend to identify themselves by adopting certain colors. The Crip gangs identify themselves with the colors blue or black or a combination of the two. Non-Crips generally use red accessories such as caps or bandanas. These color conventions are generalities and like other conventions of black gang members, are not strictly adhered to. Still, the conventions do exist and are part of the gang subculture. What sometimes makes matters more difficult is that the mere wearing of such colors does not necessarily identify the wearer as a gang member, but the individual's use of the colors may be significant inasmuch as it would be quite difficult for the wearer not to understand what the colors and modes of dress symbolize.

STONER GANGS

A recent development in the gang scene is the solidfying of lower and middle-class youth into static groups who refer to themselves as

"Stoners." The term has been used by teenagers since the early 1970's. This label was normally a reference to neighborhood groups of youth that were such persistent abusers of drugs or alcohol that they appeared to be intoxicated (i.e., "stoned" or "loaded") at every opportunity—hence the terms "Stoners" or "Loadies" were applied to them by their "square" teen peers.

The term is generically applied to groups of youth who socialize together regularly to abuse drugs and alcohol. The group's common-bond is "heavy metal" rock music. Authorities have been reluctant until very recently to classify Stoner groups as street gangs. This was primarily due to the lack of involvement of Stoners in violent activity commonly associated with street gangs. Unfortunately, as is frequently the case when young people band together and participate in anti-social behavior, they began to conflict with others around them. This behavior, as we have discussed, has the very characteristics those earlier social scientists found that produced street gangs.

Even this grouping and minor conflicts with others might have gone unnoticed had not many of the Stoners begun to exhibit many bizarre behavioral traits that drew law enforcement's attention to them specifically. One of the more obvious and peculiar traits that manifested itself was the practice of Satanism by a small segment of the Stoners. Grave robbing, desecration of human remains and churches began to occur, and the resulting investigations revealed that, at least in some cases, members of the Stoners were involved.

Figure 3.6 Shows Stoner street gang graffiti proclaiming that "Satan is here."

This scrutiny by authorities also revealed other heretofore unnoticed behavior patterns that pointed directly to Stoner involvement in street gang activity.

Traits

Certain common behavior patterns were observed by investigators. The individuals within the Stoner groups have adopted a mode of dress and appearance very unlike that of traditional gang members. They seem to favor colored T-shirts with decals of their rock music heroes or bands. Levi's and tennis shoes are also popular. The members will many times adorn themselves with metal-spiked wrist cuffs, collars and belts. Other popular items of jewelry worn by Stoners are Satanic relics or sacreligious effigies, particularly anti-Christian items.

The Stoner is also dissimilar from traditional gang members in physical appearance. He is more apt to favor the wearing of earrings, his hair will usually be shoulder length, and he will not be as prone to tattoo the body as street gang members do.

Traits in Common

Recent scrutiny of the Stoner groups indicates that they and the street gangs have many more common characteristics than contrasting ones. Both use graffiti to mark territory, but with a slightly different meaning to the word territory. Whereas street gang members claim physical portions of a community, the Stoner group will claim certain musical groups or types of music only as an ideology and occasionally, physical territory.

Street gang members have a distinctive type of dress, and as discussed earlier, the Stoners have also adopted a particular dress style. Although, obviously, different from the street gang's dress, the same motivating purpose—identity—is the reason for members of a group adopting a similar attire. The rock music, T-shirt and heavy metal accessories cater to the Stoners' ego just as the *Cholo* dress serves the street gang members' ego and sets them apart from others of their age group.

While most street gang members tend to be poor students, come from economically depressed households, and have little self-esteem, Stoners usually have directly opposing traits. The Stoners lean toward much higher scholastic achievement than do street gang members. The families of Stoners also tend to be of a higher economic status than that of street gang members—hence, the economic deprivation that faces many gang members is lessened considerably for the Stoner. Due to these factors, his self-esteem is usually healthier than that of the typical street gang member. Although these differences are appreciable, they serve the same purpose as do those of the street gang in giving a certain commonality to the Stoner.

The Stoners are also similar to street gangs in that they have adopted names for their particular groups; however, the term Stoner is not always used in the name. The terms "Freaks," "Boys," or a favorite rock group may be substituted.

To date there is little evidence of open conflict with established street gangs except for occasional flare-ups. On the contrary, what has happened is that many of the Stoner groups that have formed in areas inhabited by established gangs have allied themselves with that gang. In some cases, they have actually been accepted into the gang en masse as a separate clique.

Figure 3.7 Example of Stoner gang clothing.

With the emergence of Stoner groups and their conformance with the established characteristics of street gangs, law enforcement agencies have begun to classify these groups as such.

CAR CLUBS

Car clubs are not generally thought of as outlaw gangs, but in some communities what began as legitimate car clubs became simply organized and highly mobile street gangs.

The term "low-rider" is usually applied equally to street gangs or car clubs. Both groups typically alter the suspension system of their vehicles so that the body of the car is only a few inches from the roadway—hence the term "low-rider." However, many legitimate car clubs find the term offensive as it has become a label for gang types, and the legitimate car club member does not want to be thus identified.

Unlike street gangs, legitimate car clubs have more formal organizations, including written constitutions, elected leaders and defined roles. Furthermore, many car club members have been found to be

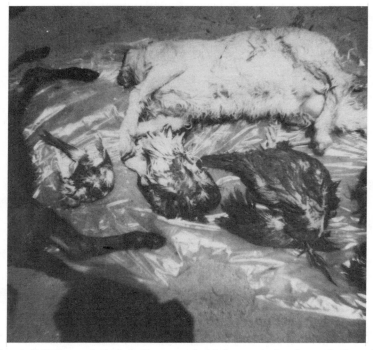

Figure 3.8 Shows beheaded goat and chickens. Animals are believed to have been used in Satanic rituals by Stoner gang.

better educated and somewhat older than their street gang counterparts. The "car clubber" is very likely to hold a job in order to support his habit—the car. Car club vehicles are expensive machines due to the extensive modification, paint jobs and other customizing work.

The car club member will go to great lengths to protect his car from damage. In the early 1970's, however, a car club war did break out in East Los Angeles. The police found that the clubs involved would shoot at, or attempt to smash their rivals' vehicles with tire tools and jacks. Many times, opposing club members would pass up an opportunity to inflict injury on a club member for a chance at the member's car.

But the outbreaks of violence involving car clubs have continued to be minimal, and most disputes are resolved to a peaceful conclusion by the members themselves. Police gang units have been most successful at negotiating with car clubs by providing a safe and secure facility for these negotiations.

Among the ploys used by car clubs is to ask local police departments to sponsor their club. However, the motive for the request for sponsorship is to gain credibility for the club at the expense of the sponsoring police department. Possibly a better procedure for a police department to follow would be to assign a liason officer to deal with all car clubs, not just one club in particular. This way a department can show concern, and at the same time not be placed in a potentially compromising position.

ASIAN GANGS

California has the largest Asian population in the continental United States. According to an article in *New West Magazine* (May 1980), one out of every two hundred Californians is a Southeast-Asian refugee. Add these people to the already established native Asian population, and the number of Oriental residents is greatly increased.

Traditionally Asians living in the United States are, as a whole, a serene and peaceful group. Crime statistics for them have always been lower than for any other cultural segment of the population. Also, Occidentals have typically ignored violence which surfaced in the Asian community, shrugging it off as part of an age-old Chinese tradition such as the Tong Wars.

Asian gangs are not generally thought of as street gangs in the usual sense, as they tend to be more organized and with an identifiable leadership. One would think on first examining the Asian gang, that it would more properly be classified as an element of organized crime.

Yet closer examination reveals that Asian gang activity has various factions, many of them utilizing the methodology of ordinary street gangs, which lacks the sophistication of organized crime. It is for this reason that the following sections on Asian gangs have been included.

Chinese Gangs

The fact is that few Tongs (secret or fraternal organizations) engage in open warfare anymore, and that most of the crimes committed in Chinatown are carried out by street gangs.

In the mid-1800's, thousands of Chinese immigrants were imported into the western United States as a cheap labor source to work primarily on the railroads—just as the Irish were brought into the eastern United States. As the Chinese population grew, and many entered into business in the Chinatowns, Tong organizations began to appear. Such organizations or fraternities began, it seems, as groups of businessmen interested in community welfare; and there probably was a substantial number of Chinese businessmen who were sincerely interested in this issue. But as is often the case, many businessmen were motivated by human greed and soon the early Tongs were involved in criminal activity and organized in much the same way as the notorious Mafia—with many of the same means and goals.

For instance, the early Tongs at the turn of the century started out as being involved in protection, gambling and vice rackets. However, wars began to break out among the Tongs over rights to exploit territories. Then as blood was shed and passions calmed and age advanced on the Tong members, they began to settle disputes, for the most part, in non-violent ways. However, occasions still arise in which the Tongs resort to violence to settle their differences.

In the early days the Tongs used "look-see" boys as lookouts for the adult Tong members. These boys were called *Wah Ching*. After a period of time, as the Tongs became more legitimate, the need for the Chings declined, but the Wah Chings themselves did not disband. They operate to this day largely taking up where the Tongs left off.

Even though the Tongs are presently primarily benevolent societies, they will, when necessary, carry out violence through the agency of the Wah Chings. Eventually, because of excessive violence, the Chinese community itself, primarily in California, spoke out against the Wah Chings. As differences of opinion developed within the Wah Ching itself, the group split into two factions: the older members became known as *Yu Li,* while the younger gang members retained the name Wah Ching. However, the formation of these groups further divided positions rather than settling them, and new violence broke out at an almost unprecedented level: open gang warfare.

The warfare was infamously commemorated when a member of the Yu Li, Joe Fong, became disenchanted with the Yu Li and further fragmented the gang by forming the Joe Fong Boys or Joe Boys. The 1967 Golden Dragon massacre that occurred at the Golden Dragon restaurant located in San Francisco's Chinatown, was a result of the Joe Fong gang attacking the Wah Ching gang which was inside the restaurant. Many people were shot during the attack and died of their wounds. However, none of those wounded were gang members, but were innocent victims caught between the two warring factions.

All three gangs (Yu Li, Joe Boys, and Wah Ching) exist today and have spread to most of the major cities of the United States and Canada. Investigators find little workable information on cases involving Chinese gangs due to the reluctance of Chinese businessmen to come forward as witnesses. As a result the gangs remain a constant threat to decent people everywhere gangs exist.

Vietnamese Gangs

Vietnamese gangs had their beginnings in the corrupt society of the Republic of Vietnam before its fall. The wave of refugees from Indo-China into the United States, brought a small but influential segment of the criminal elements as well as some opportunistic former military officers.

Upon arriving in the United States, these groups immediately set about establishing themselves within the Vietnamese community. Their *modus operandi* was very similar to that of the Chinese gangs in that the newly formed Vietnamese gangs began operating extortion rings directed at other Vietnamese. As they learned the American system of government, the gangs quickly expanded their operations into welfare fraud and auto theft.

A large percentage of Vietnamese are of Chinese ancestry and are fluent in the Cantonese Chinese dialect. The Vietnamese can and do join the Chinese street gangs. Recently, there has been some indication of Vietnamese and Chinese gangs fighting each other for territorial rights of operations.

Since the Vietnamese gangs are a relatively new phenomenon in this country, information as to their exact origins and methods is still being developed. But this much is clear: The gangs are deadly and serious about their business. They are a force to be reckoned with. As with other Asian gangs, they will be present for some time before law enforcement becomes concerned with them. Agencies would be well advised to keep an "ear to the ground" in their respective Vietnamese communities, for gang activities.

The three most powerful gangs in California are the Wah Ching, the Paratroopers, and the Frogmen. They are centered in Orange and Los Angeles Counties, but operate statewide. Moreover, more gangs are sprouting up to challenge these three—with names like Black Dragons, Pink Knights, and Lunes. Generally, however, Vietnamese gangs are beginning to adopt gang names that relate to the leader's name or nickname.

Filipino Gangs

Other Asian communities are similarly plagued by street gangs. Though not as well known nor as large as many Hispanic, black or Chinese gangs, their destructive impact within the communities where they exist is still as formidable. For instance, Filipino neighborhood street gangs are similar in structure and operation to Hispanic groups. As a result they gravitate toward Mexican gangs in their associations and friendships. The main branches of Filipino gangs are in San Francisco and Los Angeles, but cities in Alaska and Washington have also experienced Filipino gang activity. The most common Filipino gangs are the Santanas, the Taboos, and the Temple Street Gang.

Japanese Gangs

The Japanese community, on the other hand, has generally not been troubled by street gangs, although the one main gang that does exist is the Japanese equivalent to the Mafia: the *Yakuza* or Japanese syndicate. This gang is highly organized and is not a usual street gang. The Yakuza member can be ordinarily identified by his distinctive tattoos and the absence of the tip of his left little finger.

The Yakuza is deeply rooted in Japanese culture and the authorities have begun a nation-wide push to neutralize them through humiliation and thus lessen their prestige and power.

The Yakuza or Boryokudan (a derogatory term applied by Japanese police) exist in many Japanese communities in the United States, but are especially active in California and Hawaii.

Korean Gangs

The Korean commmunity has two very active gangs. The foremost is called "The Korean Killers." This gang is typical of other Asian gangs mentioned in this chapter in terms of viciousness, but is unique in that it is primarily a theft oriented gang. It operates largely throughout the Los Angeles area and in surrounding counties, burglarizing the homes of fellow Koreans. One unusual turn that this gang has taken is that it utilizes a Korean telephone directory, published by Korean businessmen, to select its victims.

The Korean Killers' main rival is a group called the "American Burgers," so named because its initial hangout was a local hamburger stand. These two gangs, like many others, often attack each other and are mutually well-practiced in the martial arts. The members are very young, usually in their teens, and they remain with their gang into adulthood.

Unlike other groups, Asian gang members do not have a particular dress code, so their gang affiliation is difficult to establish on sight. The Asian gang member, while prone to violence, is generally polite to police officers and is adept at leading one to believe that he is a student and not a threat to the community. Though well-schooled in the martial arts and a particular threat to the patrol office, the gang member generally has high respect for authority and the officer can use his status to his own advantage when the occasion arises.

PRISON GANGS

In the early 1960's a new phenomenon was spawned in the California prison system—highly organized prison gangs. These groups were so secret and well-organized that the prison system was undermined and control wrested from prison officials before the authorities were aware of their existence.

One factor that promoted the growth and spread of such gangs is the inbred violence that caged men perpetrate on each other. Racial violence has always been a serious problem within prisons, and gang organizers used racial conflicts to instigate tension and encouraged racial segregation to facilitate the growth of gangs.

Another contributing factor was the Prisoner Rights Reform Movement. Under the guise of prison reform, inmate organizers spread the word of their organization by using their attorneys or by pressing for transfers for themselves to other prisons within the system. Thus, by moving from prison to prison, not only were gangs established, but also a system for conveying information to brother gangs and further developing power by ensuring that the gang's violence could be carried out against any inmate within the penal system. No one within prison walls would be safe from gang assassinations, beating and intimidation.

The Mexican Mafia

The first and most notorious prison gang is the Mexican Mafia (EME). Organized in the late 1950's by a group of Mexican-Americans, its purpose was to protect fellow Hispanic prisoners from racial violence within the prison system. This gang is responsible for the majority of narcotics trafficking in the prisons that it controls, and employs time-honored racketeering techniques such as protection and loan sharking to develop its strength in the prison system.

The Mexican Mafia also operates outside prison walls, primarily in the urban areas of the southwestern United States. Although born in California prisons, it is a major distributor of heroin in Arizona, Nevada, New Mexico and Texas. Many narcotics-related murders in these states can be directly attributed to this group. EME will eliminate its competition in any manner possible as narcotics is its major income source.

Nuestra Familia

The Mexican Mafia's most dreaded enemy, the *Nuestra Familia* ("Our Family"), is also its major competitor. This gang, too, was born in the California prison system. According to prison officials, the Nuestra Familia was organized in 1967 at Soledad Prison. It began as a political organization whose purpose was to push for prison reform using whatever tactics, fair or foul, that were available or necessary.

The Nuestra Familia, unlike its mortal enemy the Mexican Mafia, has a written constitution and an identified rank structure from warrior to general. A favorite method for gaining promotion within the ranks is for a member to kill an enemy of the organization whose name has been published on the Nuestra Familia contract or murder "hit" list.

The Nuestra Familia openly wars with the Mexican Mafia in and out of the prison system. As the Nuestra Familia grew and became powerful, it became serious competition for the Mexican Mafia and violence occurred. The violence has now escalated to such a degree that prison officials attempt to segregate Nuestra Familia and Mexican Mafia from one another by assigning the members to separate prisons. Nevertheless, members of each gang continue to murder each other in their quest for total power and in their ambition to dominate the lucrative narcotics traffic.

The majority of Nuestra Familia recruits are prisoners committed to the prison system from rural areas, hence the nickname—"Farmers"—given them by other inmates. Once released from prison, the Farmers tend to control the narcotics and organized criminal activity in the rural areas of California. Their counterparts in the Mexican Mafia generally come from the urban areas and control similar criminal activities in the cities. This arrangement would seem to lessen the potential for direct conflict between the two Mexican gangs.

Black Prison Gangs

The Black Guerrilla Family (BGF) is a gang whose beginnings in prison were motivated by political ideals. Inside the prison, the BGF is an adjunct of the Black Liberation Army (BLA) which operates as a Marxist-Leninist terrorist organization on the streets of America. The BGF is responsible for most of the assaults on prison officials, and on several occasions has murdered prison staff. Furthermore, the organization is controlled by a central committee, with generals, captains, lieutenants, and soldiers carrying out orders from their commanders.

Even though the BGF is very strong inside prison, it is not as well-organized on the outside. This is due, at least in part, to its political terrorist nature. As the radical movement waned in the late 1970's, so did the political involvement of the BGF and BLA. The organization is now almost totally a criminal group trafficking in narcotics both within and outside prison walls. However, when members are arrested or charged with a crime, they maintain that they are being "persecuted" for political reasons.

White Prison Gangs

The Aryan Brotherhood (AB) is the most important white gang in the prison system. When first formed it called itself the Blue Bird Gang, later changing its name to Aryan Brotherhood. The members can be identified by a tattoo of the anti-Christ symbol in the form of the triple six (666) contained within a cloverleaf. The gang was formed in the early 1960's as a white supremacy group whose purpose was to protect white inmates from other racially-oriented, non-white gangs. The fervor of the gang comes from Nazi idealism which exists among white power groups that afflict certain segments of society. The Aryan

Brotherhood is composed primarily of individuals who, on the outside, associate with or belong to various white racist groups. It is particulary violent and holds a strong attraction for the violence-prone individual.

While allowing only white members, the gang has aligned itself with the Mexican Mafia in its battle to control narcotics trafficking in the prisons. Their mutual hatred of black prisoners provides a strong bond. Many of the inter-racial murders committed in the prison system are directly related to the Aryan Brotherhood and the Mexican Mafia attacking or being attacked by the BGF or the Nuestra Familia, or both. The Aryan Brotherhood hires out, or "contracts", its services for murder and other violence both inside and outside prison. However, the gang is not particularly strong outside prison because upon release, members to tend to rejoin their original white power groups or resume former criminal associations.

The gang in a prison is controlled by a general. Approval for membership is put to a vote by the gang, and advancement is obtained by committing violent acts. The more violent an individual's behavior, the more likely he is to ascend in the hierarchy.

RELATIONSHIP OF PRISON GANGS TO STREET GANGS

Essentially there is no formal relationship between these two kinds of gangs, in the sense that one is an extension of the other. However, from the evidence available, it appears that the street gang member is potential raw material for the prison gang. The majority of prison gang members were at one time members of either *barrio,* ghetto, or motorcycle gangs. The only other fact that is significant here is that since neighborhood ties are stronger for most prison gang members than prison ties, the average ex-convict rejoins the group he belonged to before entering prison.

Prison Gang Philosophy

Prison gang philosophy is very often diametrically opposed to that of the street gang. For example, although loyalty is a prime value for both groups, disagreements among prison gang members are many times settled by the murder of the offending member or members of his family. The killing of a "homeboy," on the other hand, is alien to most street gangs; and when a street gang makes raids on rival gangs, the intent is not to commit murder per se, but to terrorize rivals. If a street gang must kill to fulfill its aims, it will—but the killing itself is secondary to the intent. In a prison gang the killing is of primary importance, with the terror, which the killing generates, an added extra. The prison gang prefers to advance its own goals. Turf and neighborhood are, for obvious reasons, of no concern. But unlike the prison gang member, the street gang member forsakes everything and subordinates his own interests to the gang that he equates with the neighborhood from which he gains his identity. For the street gang member, the neighborhood and the gang which protects it are entities from which he draws sustenance. This symbiotic relationship between neighborhood, gang and individual member is particularly characteristic of Hispanic gangs whose existence, as discussed earlier, may go back so far that parents and even grandparents, in some instances, are a part of the territory in which the young gang member lives and which he helps defend from outsiders

The prison gang is different: It is cold, calculating and purposeful. Individuals who break prison gang rules are punished ruthlessly and swiftly.The street gang, on the other hand, operates through pure emotion. Its planning is usually unsophisticated, its actions spontaneous. Frequently there may not be a specific person selected as a victim. The strike will be against *any* member of the opposing gang, as the target is not an individual but the gang itself. An attack on any gang member, therefore, is an attack on the body of the gang as a whole. Any member will do.

Prison Gang Recruitment

A street gang member is too undisciplined and unsophisticated to be recruited directly into a prison gang. Therefore, prison gangs, with rare exception, seldom recruit from the street. The prison gang will wait until the youthful offender has progressed through the juvenile justice system—from probation camps, reforms schools and finally to prison. At this point the recruit has become wise in the ways of penal institutions and has matured sufficiently to be recruited into the prison gang. In today's justice system, only the worst of a very bad lot are sentenced to state prison, and they are the types that the prison gang is seeking.

In California, reform schools are called Youth Training Schools. The three main schools are located at Preston, Chino, and Norwalk. It is at these institutions that officials find young offenders beginning to affiliate with prison gangs and declaring their sympathies for certain ones. Generally those sentenced to Youth Training Schools at Chino or Norwalk will sympathize with the Mexican Mafia, as these youths tend to come from urban areas. Those sentenced to Preston affiliate with the Nuestra Familia, having come from rural backgrounds.

A Developing Rift

A phenomenon which both youth authorities and prison officials have noticed recently is a rift between prison gangs and the street gang members, in that the latter seem to be achieving an independence from the prison gangs. It appears that though young offenders continue to join prison gangs when behind bars, geographically based loyalties and animosities persist. This schism is most noticeable among Hispanic groups. Those from Northern Califonia tend to associate only with other Northerners, and those from Southern California, with members from that area. Old street rivalries are still a problem within these groups, but many times these rivalries are put aside in support of the geographic groups. Inmates from the North will sign their letters with a symbol for that area: the Spanish word *Norte,* the letter "N", or the number 14. Those from the South will write the Spanish *Sur* (south) or the number 13.

Prison gangs try to discourage such rivalry between North and South, street gang vs. street gang. This attitude on the part of prison gangs serves to alienate street gang members, as they may have been warring with a particular rival that was their gang's enemy in their grandfathers' time, and they have no intention of relaxing their traditional warfare for the benefit of the prison gang.

Because street gang members have this attitude, prison officials have found that more and more street gang members are maintaining their barrio identity even in prison. Some prisons are reporting that a number of street gangs have so many members at a particular institution that they are a force in themselves. In fact, black street gangs manage to keep their identity so well that the various factions of the Crips gangs, for example, blend with one another and present a solid front of "Crips" against all other black gangs.

It appears that only a small number of street gang members sent to prison from Southern California join the prison gang system. This does not mean that the street gang members from that area do not cooperate or sympathize with prison gangs. They do. But they become de facto members without actually joining.

Most street gang members from the urban areas of Southern California that are "official" members of prison gangs, are usually related by family ties, through blood or marriage, to prison gang members. Often these family connections influence the street gang member to affiliate himself with his kin's prison gang, particularly if the relationship is in his immediate family. When the street gang member is sentenced to prison—and prior to his arrival—the prison grapevine will generally have identified him as to his street gang affiliation, offense, and prison gang sympathies, if any. He will be observed and judged by his peers, then pressured to join or associate with a gang. For his own protection the street gang member usually affiliates with a gang that a member of his family belonged to while in prison. Otherwise, he simply gravitates toward those prison gangs which most nearly conform to his own values and ethnic background.

A certain percentage of these young men do become hard-core prison gang members, but the majority maintain their street gang identification. However, once a street gang member joins a prison gang and begins to perform for it, he tends to drift away from his neighborhood gang. As he is gradually absorbed into his new association, his influence in his original group begins to dissolve (although he will still retain the respect of the street gang for his past deeds).

Although on occasion active prison gang members will use street gang members as runners or lookouts, no evidence has been uncovered to support the claim that street gang members are employed as contract "hit men" for prison gangs, as has been widely rumored by elements within the justice system. Although the reverse has not been found to be true either, it would seem the street gang member is simply not sophisticated enough to perform in the cold, calculated manner required by the prison gang.

Since prison gangs generally thrive on anonymity they cannot afford to become involved in any way in neighborhood street gang wars, nor can they lend support to any gang outside prison walls. For instance, there were a few occasions where the Mexican Mafia was associated with street gangs, but so much opposition was generated from within the Mexican Mafia itself, the relationship was ended. The prison gang did not want the notoriety it was receiving. Thus the rift between street gang and prison gang was intensified.

Rural Street Gangs

Be that as it may, in rural areas of California a closer association exists between the local street gangs and the Nuestra Familia than exists between the Mexican Mafia and big city street gangs. This association can be accounted for, in part, because rural gangs are generally not as old or established as urban gangs. They are smaller in terms of number of gangs and the number of members. *Barrios* in rural areas tend to be smaller than in the cities, and most residents of those neighborhoods know one another. When a youth from a rural area is sentenced to prison, he is looked upon by his urban counterparts as a country "bumpkin." Chances are he will not be as worldly as they are, and will be easier to manipulate. It is also more likely that the rural youth will know a member of the Nuestra Familia personally. Thus, because of his relative lack of experience, he will seek the protection and guidance of the prison gang.

In addition, the link between the Nuestra Familia and rural street gang is made strong because the Nuestra Familia controls the flow of narcotics. If deals are to be made they must be approved by it. Among urban street gangs the existence of many independent dealers limits the control which the Mexican Mafia can exercise.

Other factors, too, enter into the picture as to the degree of control prison gangs can exert over street gangs. Law enforcement officials in both Central and Northern California have found that Nuestra Familia exercises more control over street gangs than does the Mexican Mafia. Officials have also observed that the quasi-military structure of the Nuestra Familia appeals to institutionalized rural youths, and such youths seem to adjust readily to the discipline. However, drawing conclusions as to why this appeal exists would go beyond the scope of this book. Such conclusions would be inferential and, therefore, speculative. What is important to note is that the appeal is there.

CHAPTER 4

GANG COMMUNICATION

NEED FOR RECOGNITION

Street gang members communicate primarily through their actions. Unlike the gangs associated with organized crime, which prefer anonymity, street gangs need and seek recognition. They want recognition not only from their community, but from rival gangs. A gang's image and reputation depend on this recognition, and are critically important to its members, because such visibility enhances their reputations. If a gang has a reputation for violence, then it will be feared by other less violent gangs, and the reputation for violence will devolve to the individual members simply through association.

Since media publicity adds to the prestige of a gang, police officials are often reluctant to identify the gangs involved in criminal activity, particularly in cases of violent crime. Generally the media centers any reporting of a crime on the crime itself, and not so much on the gang that committed it. Although it is not especially interesting to society as a whole which gang is involved in a crime, publicity gained from the news media is important to gang members. Many keep scrapbooks of newspaper clippings documenting their gang's exploits.

VERBAL COMMUNICATION

Verbal, as well as non-verbal, gang communication is ever present and takes a variety of forms. Letters written to fellow gang members

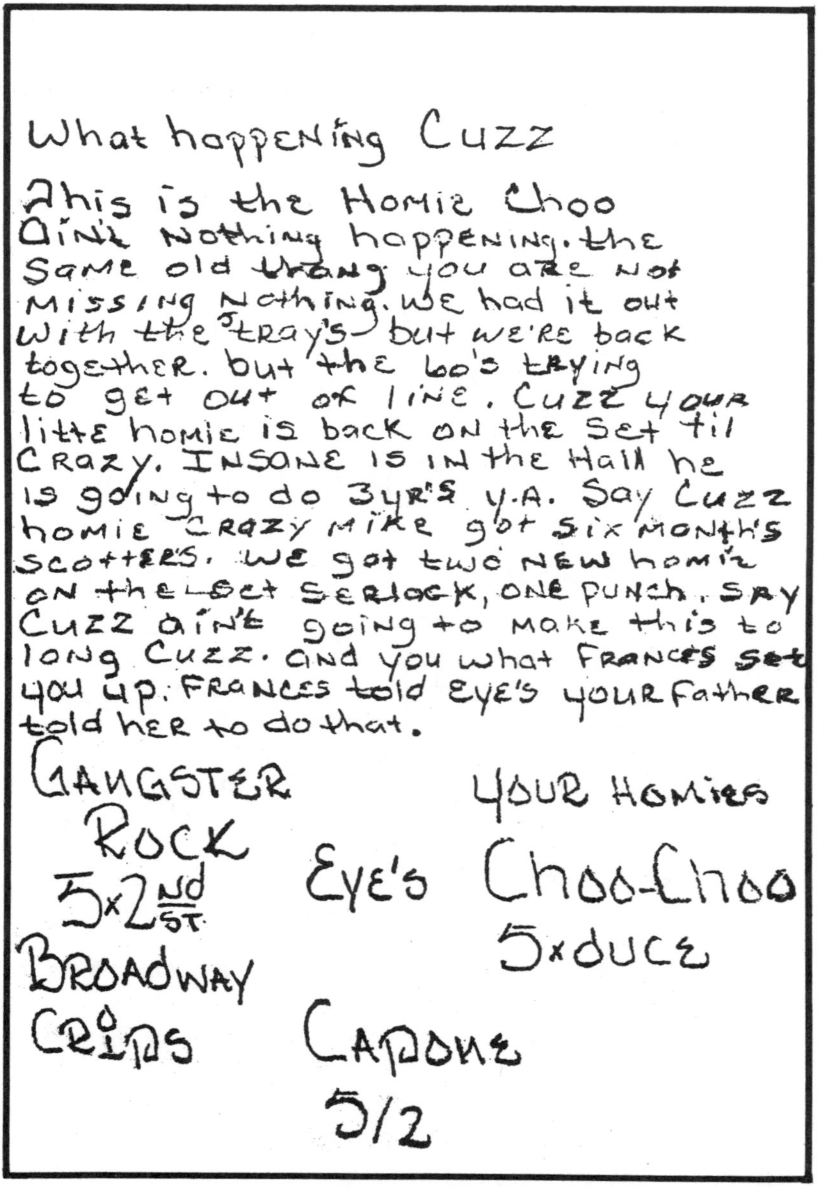

What happening Cuzz

This is the Homie Choo
Aint Nothing happening. the
Same old thang you are Not
Missing Nothing. We had it out
With the trays. but We're back
together. but the bo's trying
to get out of line. Cuzz your
litte homie is back on the Set til
Crazy. INSONE is in the Hall he
is going to do 3yr's y.A. Say Cuzz
homie Crazy Mike got six month's
Scotters. We got two New homie
on the set Serlock, one punch. Say
Cuzz aint going to make this to
long Cuzz. and you what Frances set
you up. Frances told eye's your father
told her to do that.

GANGSTER   YOUR HOMIES
 ROCK   Eye's Choo-Choo
5x2ND   5xduce
ST.
BROADWAY
CRIPS   CAPONE
              5/2

Figure 4.1 Typical letter from a gang member in prison to another gang member outside. Note gang vernacular and stylized printing.

in prison recount their gang's recent exploits, and the feats of their associates are often described in great, but exaggerated, detail. These letters are frequently written in gang vernacular, and painstakingly printed in stylized gang script. Another form of gang communication, and certainly the most observable, is the writing on walls: graffiti.

GRAFFITI

Inscriptions in the form of graffiti can be found in every large city in the United States. It is not a new method of communication, and in California gang graffiti can be traced back to the early 1940's. The messages seen today are a continuation of that tradition and vary from the innocent declarations of love for a sweetheart to the anti-establishment slogans of radicals and revolutionaries. However, most metropolitan graffiti is the work of street gangs. The bulk of this gang graffiti, especially in the Greater Los Angeles area, is written by Hispanic and black gang members. Their graffiti styles differ, not so much in the basic mechanics or meanings, but in sophistication and intensity. The primary reason for this difference is that black gangs lack the traditional gang philosophy common in the established Hispanic gangs.

The choice of lettering style illustrates these differences. While Hispanic gangs prefer stylized script-type letters, black gangs favor a much simpler "string" block-type lettering. It is called "Philly style," because of its similarities to graffiti found in Philadelphia. (The name does not imply any connection between the black gangs in Los Angeles and those in Philadelphia.)

Hispanic Gang Graffiti

Graffiti is an important part of Hispanic gang tradition. These gang members call their inscriptions *plaquesos,* or *placas.* The slang term, *plaquesos,* is derived from the Spanish, *placa,* meaning "a sign" or "plaque." When gang members talk of writing on a wall they call it "throwing a *placa* on a wall." It is not just graffiti. It proclaims to the world the status of the gang and offers a challenge to rivals.

Moreover, graffiti writing is a structured, acquired skill. It takes a great deal of time and practice to perfect the Hispanic style of wall writing. In some areas, children begin learning it at an early age and it can be found on notebooks, school papers, bus benches, tennis shoes,and even matchbook covers. Only when a writer's skill is perfected does he attempt larger structures, i.e., walls, buildings, fresh concrete, billboards and fences. No suitable surface is safe from graf-

Figure 4.2 Typical Black gang graffiti. Note plain lettering.

fiti. Tall buildings and freeway overpasses offer only a moderate challenge to a determined graffiti writer. He uses knives, chalk, paint, oil, crayons, and occasionally blood to print his message. However, cans of spray-paint and marking pens are the tools most frequently used. Quality and style are important too, because such efforts will create or enhance both the gang's image and the writer's personal status within the gang.

Although some graffiti can qualify as artistic endeavors, most scrawlings lack social appeal and may defy translation by individuals not familiar with gang communication and symbolism. The primary purpose of this discussion is not so much to focus on the visual aspects of graffiti, although examples are given, but to examine their meanings and implications.

Elements of Hispanic Gang Writing

In studying graffiti itself, certain basic elements can be discovered. For example, the main body of the writing usually contains the gang's name or logo. A logo is a descriptive emblem used to identify the gang. It may be a group of Roman numerals, initials representing the gang name, or a picture or symbol (*See Figure 4.5*). Major business

Figure 4.3 Typical Hispanic gang graffiti. Note highly stylized writing.

Figure 4.4 Depicts bus bench graffiti painted by young gang member.

corporations use logos for the same purpose: identification. Near the logo will be the *placa* (the nickname or street name) of the writer or author of the inscription. Frequently, assertions of the gang's strength and power will be stated, using such expressions as *rifa* ("to rule"), or *controllo* (a declaration of control over the area or turf). Often, gang writings will be concluded with the initials *c/s*, which stand for *con safos*, ("the same to you"). This has also been said to mean: "under penalty of death, do not mark over this inscription." Another closing inscription is *p/v*, (for *por vida*), a reference to the length of time the gang will be in control of the turf: forever.

Reading an Area's Graffiti

Much valuable information, relative to police work, can be gained by reading and understanding graffiti. One can determine what gang is in control of a specific area by noting the frequency of the un-challenged graffiti, because "throwing a *placa*" on a wall announces the claiming of a territory. When the writing is left unchallenged, it reaffirms the gang's control. Normally, the closer one moves toward the center of a gang's area, the more unchallenged graffiti can be found. Conversely, as one moves away from that center or core area,

Figure 4.5 Typical street gang logo.

the more rival graffiti and "cross-outs" are observed.

Thus, if one gang has its graffiti on a building crossed out by graffiti of another gang, it would indicate the location is contested. A "cross-out" is a type of asterisk that covers a rival's graffiti, and in gang jargon is called a "*puto* mark." Many times the words "*puto*" or "*rata*" are scribbled next to, or near, the crossed out graffiti. Lines are frequently drawn from such written insults and stand as a challenge to the gang which had its graffiti defiled. At times the *puto* is not written in the careful gang script, but sloppily, as if to emphasize contempt. Contested areas are common, and when members of both gangs arrive at the same place at the same time, a confrontation occurs. Homicides have resulted when gang members were caught desecrating a rival's territory with their own graffiti. Grafitti can also reveal which members comprise the active portion of a gang, especially its younger members.

When a gang maintains undisputed control over an area or location for an extended period of time, it is considered its turf. Gangs acquire territory in three ways: (1) they fight for it, (2) it was left to them, or

Figure 4.6 Graffiti reads: "Lil Spooky, Alpine, R." Lil Spooky is the person who wrote the graffiti. Alpine is the gang's name. The "R" denotes power.

Figure 4.7 Graffiti showing "cross-out" by rival gang member. "*Ratas*" means rats.

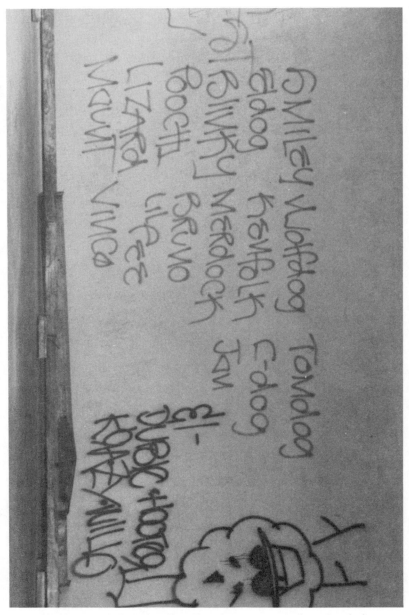

Figure 4.8 Graffiti showing list of active gang members by their street names.

(3) nobody wants it. Regardless of how a gang established its territories, in the center of its turf, safe from rivals' graffiti and cross-outs, murals can be found illustrating the gang's self-image and lifestyle. Many of these are elaborate and quite artistic. In this same core area will be the *placas* of individual gang members. A single, highly skilled graffiti writer will design and paint the gang's name or logo, and a complete list of the active members by their street names. It is not uncommon to find a list of fifty or more gang names drawn in neat rows under the gang's logo. At times it will show the order of importance, with the leaders' names first or across the top.

Wall writings are also found in the core area that record the various subfactions or "cliques" of the gang. Street gangs are composed of various factions, divided generally by age. Although not a formal organization chart, such listings do indicate how the writer views the gang's structure and who the active gang members are at the time.

Black Gang Graffiti

Black gangs use graffiti in much the same way as the Hispanic gangs. However, it is evident that there are vast differences between the two. Black gang graffiti lacks the flair and attention to detail that characterizes the Hispanic (*See Figure 4.9*).

Black gang graffiti began to appear in the early 1970's. It was very crude, but has been refined in recent years. Much of it is loaded with profanity and expressions of individual power, in contrast to the expressions of group or gang power found in Hispanic graffiti. Symbolism is obvious and crude drawings of weapons are often seen. The authors have noted that in some of the correctional institutions, Hispanic inmates will teach black gang members the finer, more delicate points of gang writing. Some of the black members, having learned this style of graffiti writing, will imitate it, but will imbue it with black gang meanings.

Stoner Graffiti

Another discernible type of graffiti that has recently appeared is that of the Stoners. Stoner graffiti differs from traditional gang writings in only a few ways. The names of heavy metal rock groups: Black Sabbath, Twisted Sister, AC-DC, and so on, have been noted. Drugs and the occult go hand-in-hand. Satanic-type drawings have been noted, which have meanings familiar only to those within the Stoner gangs. Common inscriptions such as "Natas Srewollof"

Figure 4.9 Typical Black gang graffiti. Note crude drawing of machine gun following words: ''Crips - Sir Rods.''

(Satan Followers, spelled backwards) are a result of the writers following disguised instructions found in some of the music. The custom of spelling words backwards began in the Satanic Church.

Stoners use symbolism in their graffiti more than any other gang. The upside-down cross with the numbers **666** at the ends, and the circle with a star in the center are frequently seen. These symbols have been publicized on record album covers, pictures of rock groups (including the groups' logos), and occult posters. The symbols are Satanic and originated in the Satanic churches. The gang names that Stoner members pick for themselves are generally demonic in nature or signify a violent, anti-social act.

Summary

Even though the general public regards graffiti as a form of vandalism, and perhaps an indication of a declining neighborhood, to a gang member such wall writing is not vandalism. It is an essential communication medium that advertises his group, describes its social structure, records its conflicts, and exalts its lifestyle.

CALO-SLANG

Gang members have set themselves apart from the rest of society by using their own systems of verbal communication, although such systems are no longer widely used. Black gangs have used a type of street language composed of slang terms that have meaning only to those that know the slang. Hispanic gangs converse in Spanish when approached by non-Hispanics, and the more hostile gangs have an argot called *calo*. An argot is a private, or secret, speech known only to members of the same group—in this case, fellow street gang members.

Gang Street Language

Calo is a Spanish that is not taught in school but learned on the streets. Though its use is not limited to any group or section of society, gang members may limit their vocabulary to the *calo*. The use of *calo* becomes important to the gang member because it is the language of the only group which holds significance for him: his gang. It is from his gang that he gains sustenance, identity, and a sense of belonging.

Because *calo* is often incomprehensible to both Spanish and English speaking persons, its use within a gang by gang members heightens their sense of separateness from society and establishes intimacy within their own sub-culture. As the *calo* terms are learned by those outside the group, the gang will devise new ones which rapidly enter common use, thus maintaining and perpetuating the gang's mystique. For example, according to gang informants, *vato loco* means, literally, a "crazy guy"; and denotes a Hispanic who steals, shoots dope, and spends some time in prison (usually in that order). If a gang member engages in any of these activities, in *calo* terminology he has officially become *vato loco,* and once so identified, as a matter of pride, will continue to behave in that manner. Thus, the label identifies the individual and directs his behavior. The implication of labelling him extends beyond identification. In fact, labels become directives for behavior and role playing. On the other hand, as *vato loco* denotes a "crazy guy," *escuadra* is the word denoting a "square" or law-abiding individual, and there seems to be no gray area between *escuadra* and *vato loco.* A person is either one or the other, but never

Figure 4.10 Stoner graffiti depicting name of "Rush" (rock group) and pentagram surrounded by number 666 (marks of Satan).

both.

Calo also includes and reflects the conditions and attitudes of the gang's neighborhood. There are many references for which no *calo* terms exist (e.g., education, religion, economics, etc.). However, *calo* does have words for activities such as eating (*refinar*), drinking (*pistiar*), fighting (*chingasos*) and dancing (*borlotear*). A gang member's almost exclusive use of *calo* tends to curtail his imagination, and through prolonged use would seem to distort his view of reality and, by extension, of society. All types of work are grouped under the derogatory epithets, *cameo* (from the Spanish, "camel") and *jale* (from Spanish, "to pull"). Whether a man has worked as a laborer in a construction gang or as a chemist in a research institute, within the *calo* structure he is still *jalando* (pulling) or *camelando* ("camelling"). Therefore, a high correlation exists between anti-social attitudes and an extensive use of *calo*. It is in *calo,* then, the language of his gang, that the member thinks and communicates.

CLOTHING

Even though the gang member uses graffiti and perhaps some form of *calo* to identify with his gang, it is equally important for him to reinforce his sense of belonging in a more direct, non-verbal way, by adopting a gang style of dress.

Most members are proud of their gang and openly display signs of membership in it—one indication being the way he is dressed. But there are exceptions. Non-gang youths may appear to dress like gang members by carrying canes, wearing certain colors, earrings, caps and the like. Or a gang member may be a kind of maverick who belongs to a gang but does not dress in a sterotypical fashion identifiable with it. The final determining factor regarding dress depends on whether the person wants to be identified as a gang member, or not.

Similar kinds of gangs dress in a like manner. Street gangs will dress in one style, while outlaw motorcycle gangs dress in another. Van or car club members, instead of dressing in a specific style, wear special jackets or sweat shirts to identify their members, as do a few of the street gangs. Oriental gangs generally blend into their surroundings and are undistinguishable in appearance to the outsider.

Types of Gang Styles

There are two basic types or categories of gang clothing. First, there is the type that will lead the observer to the conclusion that the wearer belongs to a gang, without specifically identifying which one. The clothing may indicate the kind of gang (street gang, biker, etc.), but not the name of the gang itself.

The second type of gang clothing does identify the gang. This is evident in areas where street gang members wear jackets or sweat shirts with their gang name or logo on the back. This type of identification is also popular with the outlaw motorcycle gangs. When members want to be thus identified with a specific gang, they will "fly colors," meaning that they wear their jackets or vests with an identifying patch or logo on the outside where it is visible. When they are not "flying colors," the jacket or vest will be worn inside-out, hiding the identification.

Outlaw Motorcycle Gangs

Each outlaw motorcycle or biker gang has its own unique emblem, and it signifies something about the gang and its self-image. Most of the gangs have adopted grotesque figures, along with a motorcycle likeness, for their emblem. The standard outfit for the biker gang is Levis, boots, Levi or leather vests or jackets (often with the sleeves cut off), earrings—and an overall dirty, unkempt appearance: long matted hair, beards, earrings, and numerous tatoos. Again, exceptions will be found, but practically all motorcycle gang members choose to dress in this fashion. The more radical, stereotyped outlaw image projected by dressing this way contrasts with that of the members of more moderate motorcycle clubs. They, too, wear logos and club insignia on their jackets and vests, but the rest of their attire lacks the "outlaw" image.

Street Gang Clothing

Street gangs, also, have two different styles. The Hispanic gang member has a more or less traditional gang uniform, while black gang members prefer individual articles to identify their gang. We should stress, at this point, that it is not the type of clothing that makes it gang clothing, but rather the way it is worn and the importance the gang member places on the "right look."

Hispanic Street Gang Clothing

The Hispanic street gang member has a distinctive appearance. He may be totally "dressed down" or "khaki'd out", or he may have only one or two badges of his gang's image. The following items of clothing are often used for this purpose:

Watchcaps:	They are generally dark blue or black in color, and knitted from wool or other material. They are worn pulled down to cover the ears, with a small roll at the bottom.
Baseball and Golf Caps:	Members may write their nicknames and that of their gang on the underside of the bill, and wear the hat with the bill turned up. Some have been observed with the gang's name or logo embroidered on the front.
Bandanas or "Moco Rags":	These are worn just over the forehead and tied in the back. They may be used as head sweatbands. The usual wearing denotes gang membership and reflect the gang's previous Indian heritage. Some gangs use black bandanas for funerals; however, the bandana can be of various colors and may have the gang or the member's name embroidered on the front.
T-Shirts:	The round or V-neck T-shirt is worn during the summer and is usually several sizes too large with the bottom worn outside the pants. The extra size allows for concealment of weapons. The over-shoulder strap undershirt is also commonly worn during the summer and is often tucked into the trousers. The gang member who is "buffed up" (muscular) favors this shirt.
Wool or Pendleton Shirts:	This type of shirt has long been associated with the traditional type of street gang. It is usually buttoned at the collar and the cuffs. The remaining buttons are left unfastened. If the shirt is not worn, it is carried reverently, neatly folded on the member's arm.
Trench Coats:	During the winter, dark trench coats are often worn, not only for protection against the elements, but to conceal weapons easily. The trench coat also makes the member seem more intimidating.

Pants:	Khaki pants, highly starched with a crease, baggy and too long, split up the side from six to eight inches above the ankle, are still popular in some gang areas. Blue jeans, also known as "counties", are worn in a similar fashion, as are gray work pants.
Suspenders and Belts:	Suspenders are, more often than not, worn down off the shoulders and trail behind the wearer. When belts are worn, they tend to be narrow.
Shoes:	Shoes range from tennis to military-type, with plain or pointed toes. If the shoes are leather, they will be smooth and highly polished. At times, sandals are worn, and generally, they are black in color with matching black socks. Tennis shoes often will have graffiti around the sole.

Black Street Gang Clothing

Although the black gangs do not follow a continuing dress style as Hispanic gangs do, they have selected certain types of distinguishing clothing and accessories for identification. Many of the items used by black street gang members were so unique that one could not only conclude that the individual was a gang member, but could even tell what gang he belonged to. For example, during the mid-1970's, members of one gang carried canes and wore only one glove (usually on the left hand). Before the practice became popular among the general public, some gang members pierced one ear and wore tie-tacks or studs in their ears. In addition, certain adornments were reserved for the gang leaders and those that excelled as gang members. Gang members also followed the trends set by their leaders, and when a leader changed styles, so did the members.

Black gang styles change rapidly, but the following items are, or have been, used by gang members to identify their affiliations:

Watchcaps:	Most often dark blue or black, and worn in a manner similar to the Hispanic gangs.
Wide Brim Hats:	Various styles have been worn. These hats often display different color bands with each gang favoring a different color.
Small Brim Hats:	Commonly called "stingybrims." These hats are not used as much today, possibly due to the variety of their styles.

Baseball & Golf Caps:	Often worn with the bill folded up or worn backwards. Graffiti is found on the underside of the bill or on the back of the inside - band.
	NOTE: During gang fights, hats, canes, or even ear studs are taken from the losers and used as spoils to increase the victor's gang image.
Hairstyles:	Hairstyles are frequently the same within the core or inner-circle of the gang. These styles include shaved heads, large naturals, superfly, corn-rolled or braided hair.
Handkerchiefs or Bandanas:	Usually very large (railroad type), generally red or blue in color and worn hanging from rear pants pocket. Once again, different colors are used by different gangs.
Shoes:	Styles vary, but tennis shoes and canvas shoes are often seen. Different colors of shoe laces have been used to distinguish the rival gangs.
Coats:	Tanker jackets and bomber-style jackets are popular and are usually black or dark blue. Trench coats also are used much in the same manner as with the Hispanic gangs. Surplus knee-length, military-type coats have also been used, with the longer coats used to hide rifles or sawed-off shotguns.

Many black gang members believed that a leather jacket was a status symbol and indicated wealth. Consequently, they would try to steal any that they found. Some of the assaults involved in the robberies ended in homicides.

As mentioned earlier, it can often be difficult to verify gang membership except through continual observation. Clothing by itself is only an indication of gang involvement, and interestingly, the dress style of the non-traditional black gang is highly individualistic and quite flexible. Early in the 1970's, gang members wore distinctive gang style regalia as they strolled along local streets, loitered on school grounds and in parks, or "hung out" at neighborhood fast-food stands. The gang clothing made it easy, when opposing gangs were looking for victims for retaliation.

When it came to the attention of the police and school officials that the gangs were frequently involved in violence, their activities were closely monitored. Members were often stopped, and after, arrested for weapons and narcotic violations. As a result of this attention, many gang members changed their dress style to one that was less conspicuous. It became common for members to carry their gang clothing and to "dress out" just prior to a gang fight.

TATTOOING

In addition to dress style, and as a peculiar kind of extension of it, gang members also tattoo themselves. Tattooing is a custom of ancient origin, and is certainly not limited to gang members or to the criminal element of any society. However, studies and field experience show that gangs use tattoos as a method of communication and identification. In this setting, tattooing is thought to be an expression of contempt for socially accepted mores. There seems to be a definite relationship between the number of tattoos an individual has and the number of times he has been confined in penal institutions. To the gang member, and especially to the youthful offender, tattooing lends status as the gang member's red badge of courage within the prison community, and serves to direct attention and prestige to him. Tattoos also serve to identify the gang members both within and outside of prison with other gang members, by showing that he not only shares gang values, but is permanently dedicated to them.

Hispanic Gang Tattooing

The traditional Hispanic gangs have used tattoos extensively, and frequently tattoo themselves with their *placa* or moniker and the name of their gang. The tattoos are usually visible on arms, hands, or shoulders. They may be as small as a homemade dot in the web of a hand, or so large that the logo covers the individual's entire back or abdomen (*See Figure 4.11*). The wearing of a gang tattoo increases the probability to about 99 percent that the wearer is a member of that gang, because for a non-member to do so will bring punishment to the imposter—beatings or even death—inflicted not only by the offended gang, but by their rivals, inasmuch as it represents an insult to the entire gang community.

Black Gang Tattooing

In contrast, black gang members are not enthusiastic about using tattoos to signify their membership, and ordinarily do not do so. One might speculate as to why black members do not choose to identify themselves in this way, but as discussed in the section on "Gang Typologies," these youths tend to be more individualistic and less inclined to identify themselves permanently with any one group.

Motorcycle Gang Tattooing

Nevertheless, most of the tattoos gang members have on their bodies relate to their gang membership since belonging to, and identification with the gang is a matter of great pride. Members of motor-

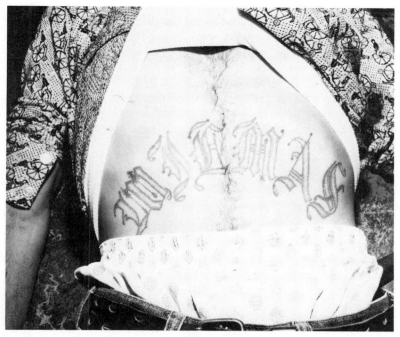

Figure 4.11 Dead gang member's tatoo reads: "Wilmas," which stands for city of Wilmington, CA.

cycle gangs are also extensively tattooed and for many of the same reasons. By displaying his tattoo, he carries the image of his gang. If the gang is feared and has a reputation for violence, the member himself may also be feared.

Tattoos of Female Gang Members

Female gang members are also tattooed, though not as extensively as are the males. Females most commonly wear small dots or crosses in the web of the hand or on the face or neck. The tattoos of the female who associates with outlaw motorcycle gangs are often marks to indicate she is the property of the gang or of an individual member. The tattoos can be found on almost any part of the body.

Meanings of Gang Tattoos

Tattoos are a personal expression of the individual who wears them. The meaning may be obvious, as in the case of a gang logo, or it may be hidden and significant only to a few. For example, the teardrop tattoo has been worn by both young adult male and female gang members. The tattoo is usually worn beneath one eye, off to the side of the face. Originally, when a male gang member wore a single teardrop tattoo, it meant that he had served time in a Youth Authority Camp or institution. When two teardrops were worn, it told everyone he had made a "hit" (killed a rival gang member). No doubt other members received the same status from the one wearing the tattoo, without necessarily meeting the criteria. In fact, some stated that each teardrop represented a killing. On the other hand, when the teardrop is worn by some of the female gang associates, it is often in memory of "homeboys" that have been killed. If a true meaning exists for this tattoo, it is elusive.

HAND SIGNS

Another non-verbal method of gang communication is the "flashing" of hand signs. The purpose of these is to identify the user with a specific gang. The signs have certain features in common with graffiti, and graffiti and gang signs are spoken of in similar terms, i.e.,members do not just write on a wall, they "throw" or "toss" graffiti on the wall. Similarly, they "throw", "toss", or "flash" gang hand signs. But whereas graffiti is often a challenge to rivals, created at night by unseen gang members, "flashing" or "tossing" hand signs is a face-to-face signalling. Confrontations frequently begin with gang signs being flashed between rivals, and soon escalate into verbal abuse and/or physical violence.

The origin of the use of gang hand signs is difficult to trace with certainty. They first drew the attention of police officials in the early 1970's, when black gang activity began its most recent increase. From 1970 to 1975, hand signs were almost exclusively a black gang feature, but in the mid-1970's, Hispanic gang members were observed flashing their gang's signs. Presently, the use of hand signs appears to be a

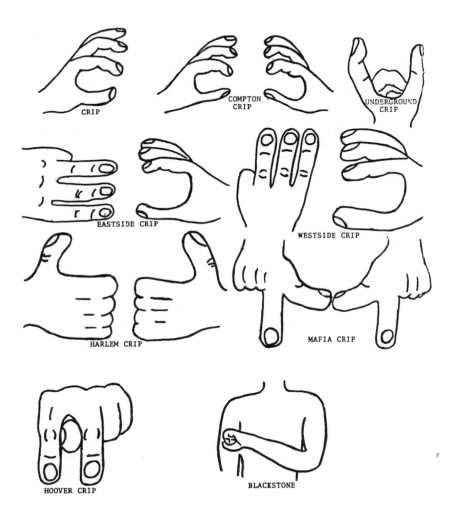

4.12a Various common gang hand signals.

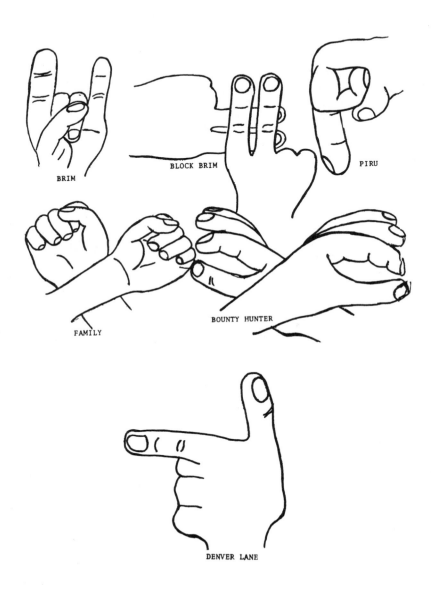

4.12b   Various common gang hand signals.

common practice among both Hispanic and black street gangs.

The actual mechanics of a hand sign may be complex or simple, depending on the name of the gang. Many black street gangs have multiple names. For example, one can use the hypothetical gang named the "Rollin', Twentieth Street, Gangster, Player, Shooters." In order to identify gangs with names such as this, multiple signs or movements are necessary. The hypothetical gang named here would require five signs or movements in order to identify each part of its name. Some of the sign movements are quite complex and time consuming, and tactical limitations soon become apparent. For instance, many gang attacks and shootings are preceded by sign flashing. The signs may take two hands to complete, so either the attacking gang member gives the sign and then goes for his gun, or he has another member do the signalling or the shooting. The limitations are obvious: The member who is doing the flashing is a target as soon as he displays his gang's sign.

Most of the gang signs in use today are simple and easily recognizable, at least to other gang members. As it is not practical to provide illustrations or photographs of the hand signs of all the active gangs, examples are given that are representative of both black and Hispanic street gangs. (*See Figure 4.12*). Additionally, gangs that have similar names or first letters may share share similar signs.

CONCLUSION

Regardless of the method of communication that gangs use, the messages are clear. The gang member is telling the world that his gang or *barrio* is number one, the best. He is expressing his total commitment to turf and gang, for it is from these that he achieves his sense of self-worth and identity. Without these, he is lost.

PART II:
POSSIBLE SOLUTIONS

INTRODUCTION TO PART II

PART II
POSSIBLE SOLUTIONS

INTRODUCTION TO PART II

It is not the intent of the authors to dictate policy to law enforcement agencies, but rather to share nearly thirty years of combined experience in dealing with the street gangs of the Greater Los Angeles Metropolitan area.

How does this experience apply in other areas and jurisdictions? In collecting information relative to street gangs throughout the western United States, the authors found one common theme: the Greater Los Angeles area seems to be the "mother city" of gangs. Investigators from other areas continually report that the gangs in their jurisdictions imitate those in Los Angeles. In many cases, the founding core members of their gangs either moved in from the Los Angeles area, or received their exposure to the world of street gangs while imprisoned with gang members from the Los Angeles area. Modern street gang activity appears to have its roots in the Los Angeles milieu, and has patterned itself after the gangs of that area. It is for these reasons that the authors offer to share their experiences so law enforcement officers everywhere will be able to present a solid front to their antagonists in the street.

Presumably, the reader can now identify the conditions that breed street gangs, the structure of the gang, and the gang members themselves. How does one utilize all this information to abate the problem in his or her area? The second part of this text is devoted to this question and to providing law enforcement approaches that have proven effective in combating street gangs' criminal activity.

CHAPTER 5

MEASUREMENT OF GANG VIOLENCE

PROBLEM IDENTIFICATION

Surprisingly, recognizing a gang problem is not as difficult as determining its magnitude and scope. Gang vandalism and graffiti can testify to the existence of a gang but not to the severity of the problem. A method must be developed which accurately measures gang violence because law enforcement agencies lack the personnel and time to direct their attention to any but what appear to be the most violent gangs. Thus, agencies face the hard task, not only of determining what activities gangs are involved in and defining the extent and nature of the problem, but also of determining how to curtail the violence and how best to protect the community in the process.

HOW SHOULD VIOLENCE BE MEASURED?

The ideal way of measuring gang crime would be to know all of the activity that each gang is involved in within a jurisdiction. However, such an approach is not practical as it is not possible to determine at all times what crime a gang is involved in. But there are practical steps which can be taken, which, while not perfect, will greatly assist in determining what crimes are gang-related.

First, gangs and their members have to be identified. Next, specific crimes must be selected and used as a constant measure of gang crime. Third, the individuals suspected of having committed a crime should, of course, be gang members—or at least thought of as having gang ties of some kind.

The first element, identificaton of the various gangs and their members, is an on-going process. The very nature of gang membership is transitory. As members gravitate away from gang involvement or are sent to jail, new, younger members join who must be identified.

The crimes selected to serve as a gauge of gang activity must be carefully chosen. For example, gang members often commit burglaries to obtain cash and guns for themselves, the gang, or both. Unless something specific indicates gang involvement—such as graffiti or a witness that identifies a gang member—the crime may not be attributed to gang activity.

Car theft also falls into this category. Using these types of crimes as a gauge of gang activty is impractical because of the difficulty in establishing a connection between a gang and a crime; and when a connection is established, the relation between the two is tenuous at best. Therefore, crimes that are consistently reported as gang-linked should be monitored closely in an empirical attempt to determine the facts. Consequently, the following crimes are often used to measure gang violence:

1. Murder
2. Assault with Attempt to Commit Murder
3. Assault with a Deadly Weapon
4. Robbery
5. Rape by Force
6. Kidnapping
7. Arson

In addition to these, some jurisdictions include as being gang-related: Shooting into an Inhabited Dwelling, Battery and Assault with a Deadly Weapon on a Police Officer, Extortion and Witness Intimidation.

In order to be considered gang-related, a monitored crime must be reported and the suspect or victim must be identified as a gang member. The identification can be direct, as in the case in which the victim or suspect is known and is listed in the agency's gang files. On the other hand, if an investigation strongly suggests that the incident involves a gang member, the crime may be classified as gang-related.

Exceptions to the foregoing occur when a gang member is a victim of one of the catalogued crimes but the perpetrator is not. In that event, a gang member is considered simply as being a random victim of crime. Interestingly, in areas where a gang crime monitoring program goes into effect, statistics relative to gang activity appear to increase in epidemic proportions. However, the apparent reported increase reflects more the systematic collection of such information, rather than an actual increase in gang crime. This tendency levels as the gang file of identified membership rolls stabilizes. Therefore it is most important that a consistent set of rules apply to determine which crimes are related or involved.

Allowing that most agencies monitor violent incidents involving gang members, one might expect a certain consistency in the level of reported activity. Unfortunately, this is not the case, and the cause for the differences is most apparent when one sees the variety of definitions as to what constitutes a gang-related crime.

Some experts feel that only when a gang acts as a unit should a crime committed by its members be considered a gang crime. Others believe that gang crime, especially violent crime, committed by individual members is of paramount importance and should be included as well. To make matters worse, reporting procedures vary across the United States. One of the largest police departments in the country has as its own policy, that gang violence, crime, etc., is to be reported as gang activity only when five or more members from a gang attack or fight with five or more members of a rival gang. Otherwise, it is reported and included with the statistics of street crime and violence in general.

In the light of the changing patterns of gang violence, needless to say this jurisdiction had relatively few violent gang crimes. The days when one gang, as a gang, would "rumble" and attack their rivals, are rare except in the world of the movies. Drive-by attacks, five to ten suspects robbing one or two victims, ambushes and snipings do not lend themselves easily to inclusion within gang crime statistics inasmuch as such crimes can be, and are, committed by individuals other than gang members. The difficulty in gathering accurate, gang-related crime statistics arises from the obvious problem of identification and definition.

Thus, many questions have to be answered and decisions made as to what criteria are to be used in reporting crime as being gang-linked: should gangs operating only as units be considered, or should a crime which an individual commits while he is a member of a gang be included? Should the criterion be the number of gang members involved? If so, how many members must be present before a crime can be included in the statistics? Should a fight between members of two gangs be included, or should a crime be listed only when the victims are non-gang members? Should a crime a member commits be counted if it is against his own family? Is that crime gang-related? Should innocent bystanders who are victims be listed as being victims of gang activity? How are accidental shootings to be catalogued?

It is acknowledged beforehand that no matter what system is adopted, someone somewhere will find a flaw in it. But what will be of enormous help is a system which, despite all its possible flaws, will at least be consistent. Consistency ensures a reliable basis for comparison and provides a means for avoiding manipulating statistics that are unrealistic or might otherwise distort the truth of what is happening within a jurisdiction, since all agencies would be using similar criteria.

CHAPTER 6

THE GANG UNIT

THE NEED FOR SPECIALIZATION

Gang violence has reached epidemic proportions and poses a serious threat to society. The insidious growth of gang activity, including both planned and unplanned gang violence, does not lend itself to either a simple or lasting solution. Even saturating a gang-impacted area with patrol forces has only a limited degree of success, and then, for just a short period of time. It is evident, therefore, that if any real progress is going to be made to secure society against the threat of gangs, it will have to be through the use of sophisticated, specialized law enforcement units, specially trained in combating those elements. The nature, size, techniques, and other matters relative to the formation of such units will depend upon the severity of the problem within the community and the resources that the community itself is willing to dedicate to solving the problem it faces.

GOALS AND OBJECTIVES

However, before a gang unit can be formed, decisions must be faced with reference to what goals and objectives can be realistically expected and attained. One foremost problem, as stated earlier, is a lack of sufficient resources, and, of course, that limitation will shape what can be done. Even so, realistic forethought and planning can go far in developing a unit which can be both efficient and cost effective.

The following is a list of typical questions which may be considered by almost any agency to use as a guide in clarifying its policies and programs for the forming of its own gang unit.

1. What will be the unit's primary function?
2. Will the unit be responsible for the criminal investigation of all gang cases?
3. Will the unit operate as a monitoring section, compiling and disseminating intelligence information?
4. Will the unit handle field enforcement operations and patrol gang areas to curtail violence?
5. Will the personnel work in plainclothes or in uniform?
6. Will the unit operate covertly, with undercover operations?
7. Will the unit function as a line or support section?
8. What will be the best hours of operation, and how many days a week should the unit be on duty?
9. Where will the unit be assigned (patrol, detective, or administrative)?

UNIT OBJECTIVES

Although the mechanics of a gang unit's operation may vary, law enforcement agencies share similar objectives. Existing gang units are typically responsible for the following:

1. To be aware of the problems of a gang-impacted area.
2. To document gang activity by monitoring gangs and their members.
3. To build, maintain, and promote gang expertise and awareness throughout the agency.
4. To use this knowledge in identifying wanted gang members, investigating cases, and assisting in the prosecution.
5. To act as a communication link, gathering and refining gang activity information, and disseminating information to officers. who are responsible for apprehending suspects and preventing gang violence.
6. To keep the command officers apprised as to gang activity, including anticipated movements.
7. To work with other jurisdictions or other parts of the criminal

justice system.

8. To work with and assist the community in its anti-gang efforts.
9. To arrest wanted gang members and gather evidence to ensure a successful prosecution.

PERSONNEL SELECTION

The selection of personnel for assignment to a gang unit is important regardless of the unit's configuration or the number of officers required. The effectiveness of a gang unit's operation will depend on the caliber of the personnel assigned. Officers should be chosen because of the capability and desire to work with a great degree of independence. However, gang units must still be structured to include a system of officers and supervisors. Although the selection of officers who work well with little or no direct supervision is desirable, many sensitive tasks are better accomplished in conjunction with supervisory personnel.

The number of personnel assigned to a gang unit will vary according to the unit's function. In those instances where a unit has investigative responsibilities, the number of detectives can be correlated to the number of cases to be investigated. The same can be done with the uniformed crime suppression officers, using measureable gang activity as a yardstick for the number of officers required. Fewer officers are needed if the unit's only responsibility is intelligence gathering. The exact number depends on the problems and goals of the gang unit. Regardless of the functions delegated to the unit, all duties and responsibilities should be clearly defined early in the development of the program.

OPERATIONS OF THE GANG UNIT

When viewing the operation of a gang unit, it is rare to find one that does not combine intelligence functions with other law enforcement activities. Some units attempt to handle the entire problem, but this approach appears to be workable only with small departments that do not have a major gang problem. Normally, because of the sheer weight of the numbers of crimes and gang members, a unit cannot effectively handle all aspects of the gang problem alone.

The gang unit must be a resource for the agency it serves. Its personnel should be experts able to answer any question relating to gang activity. To accomplish this, the officers have to spend much of their time in the gang areas, monitoring the criminal activity and talking with street gang members. Along with this, the officers should examine crime and arrest reports to learn if any of the reported incidents are gang-related. Each gang unit will have to decide what criteria to use in determining if a specific incident is gang-related. All this information must not only be compiled, but recorded so that statistically its significance, or lack thereof, may be quickly and efficiently assessed in determining the relevancy of such information to gang activity.

ADMINISTRATIVE CONTROLS

Administrative controls are necessary to ensure the smooth operation and attainment of the unit's goals. Logs, statistical reports, crime trends, and intelligence information add to the value and credibility of the unit and, thus, must be scrupulously maintained. Definite guidelines must be established showing the goals of the unit, the operating procedures, and the duties of assigned personnel. These guidelines, policies, and procedures should be reviewed periodically and revised as necessary to stay abreast of the times.

DISSEMINATION OF GANG INFORMATION AND LOG MAINTENANCE

Information critical to controlling and suppressing gang activity often becomes even more valuable when shared. Inquiries from law enforcement personnel requesting information should be documented and logged for future reference. This log serves as an administrative aid that will control the flow of information. It should be maintained on a chronological basis, and each request for information should include the following:

1. The date and time the information was received.
2. The source of the information.
3. The name of the officer receiving the information.
4. The information itself, including the names of the gangs and/or members involved, and the probable location, date, and time of the activity.

A problem inherent in many specialized units is a one-way flow of information. Some information has only intelligence value and should be stored for future use. However, most information pertaining to gangs must be acted upon quickly. Consequently, the following must also be logged:

1. The name of those notified about the information
2. The action taken in reference to the information.
3. Results of the action taken.

COOPERATION BETWEEN AGENCIES

Since gangs do not exist solely within city or county boundaries, and since gang clashes all too frequently involve more than one jurisdiction, it helps to know what gangs are active or reside in adjacent areas or jurisdictions. Even though the task is demanding, it is imperative for an officer to be informed as to which gangs are active in his or her own jurisdiction. It is more difficult to have other than a general knowledge of which gangs are active in neighboring jurisdictions. To keep informed it is necessary to maintain a good working relationship and have an effective information exchange arrangement with gang units of other law enforcement agencies.

GANG FILES

Though many issues are involved in the formation of any specialized gang unit, the basic structure of such a unit must include files which can efficiently store, retrieve, and disseminate information about gangs and gang members. These files are an integral part of the operation of the unit and provide an essential tool for law enforcement.

What to Include

Alphabetical listing of gangs and their membership is, of course, a basic requirement for any system. However, mere names alone, listed alphabetically, are not enough. Photographs of gang members, the types of crime that each gang typically commits, the individuals within each gang identified as to the kind of crime they tend to commit, their leadership roles, along with brief anecdotal records denoting evidence or some kind of substantiation as to what specific crime(s) an individual may be linked, are also needed. How deeply the gang may be involved will combine with the above to provide an accurate view of the problem faced within a jurisdiction. The volume and specific type of information that an agency may wish to include in its file is determined by the circumstances and magnitude of the gang problem an agency faces.

Groups Which Should Be Included in the File

Any group of individuals who consistently band together and have an identity as a group, who pose police and community problems, and who can be considered as a gang (using the criteria defining a gang given in Chapter 2) should be be included in a gang file. However, van and car clubs should be entered into the file only after ascertaining that such groups function as gangs. To include even small street groups without evaluating the permanency of their organization, threat to the community, or level of activity is usually a waste of time.

Criteria for Name Entry into Gang Files

The gang file should contain the names of known gang members and associate members. Generally, the two types of members differ only in the degree to which actual gang membership can be substantiated. Certainly one of the more controversial aspects of police gang files stems from the criteria used to determine whether or not an individual is a gang member. Actually, this is relatively simple. Most gang members freely admit membership, and many are fiercely proud of their gang. However, some gang members, for a variety of reasons, refuse to acknowledge their affiliation. In these situations, other relevant features must be examined to determine if the individual is a gang member. Tattoos, clothing, demeanor and statements from associates and victims are useful in determining this.

Parent Notification

When juveniles (under eighteen years of age) are identified as being gang members or associates, and their names are put into police gang files, their parents or guardians should be contacted. The circumstances of the juvenile's gang involvement and activity should be explained to the parents. Making the parents aware of the violent realities of their child's gang involvment is advisable. It may frighten them, as it should, into taking control, or, if such is not possible, seeking help to redirect the juvenile's activities.

TYPES OF GANG FILES

Each law enforcement agency facing a gang problem must determine the kind of gang file system that will best serve its needs. Most agencies adopt a system modified from the following examples.

Gang File

Each gang should be filed by name separately and alphabetically. In jurisdictions with a large number of gangs, it may be useful to further subdivide them according to type: i.e., motorcycle, prison, car club, etc.

Some agencies have developed a gang biography card to profile each gang. These are filed with the described gang and should include as much of the following information as possible.

1. The number of active and associate members.
2. The type of gang it is (street, motorcycle, car club, etc.).
3. The ethnic composition of the gang.
4. The gang's territory and boundaries.
5. The gang's hideouts.
6. The type(s) of crime(s) the gang member usually commits.
7. The gang's method of operation (M.O.).
8. The gang's choice of victims (illegal aliens, the aged, etc.).
9. The members who fill leadership roles.
10. The members who are known to be violent.

The Gang Member File

Each card should contain the member's name, physical description, addresses, and other relevant identifying data, such as tattoos, names of associates, and locations where he has been contacted or arrested, and—most importantly—a recent photograph, when possible. Each card should also have the dates of police contact or arrests and a synopsis of each contact. In addition, the identity of the officers making the entry is essential. The card should also state how the subject was identified as a gang member. If he admitted to being a member, include the name of the officer or detective who received the admission and when it was given. Always include information that indicates the subject is known to be violent, armed or combative with the police, if such is true (*See Figures 6.1 and 6.2*).

The Gang Member Pointer File

A pointer file connects the name of the suspected gang member with the more complete card filed under the name of the gang. This is an alphabetically arranged cardex file, containing the name, address, physical description, moniker (nickname) or alias, and gang affiliation of the subject. The information on the card in addition to the subject's name, is needed to reduce problems when searching the file and running across similar names (*See Figure 6.3*).

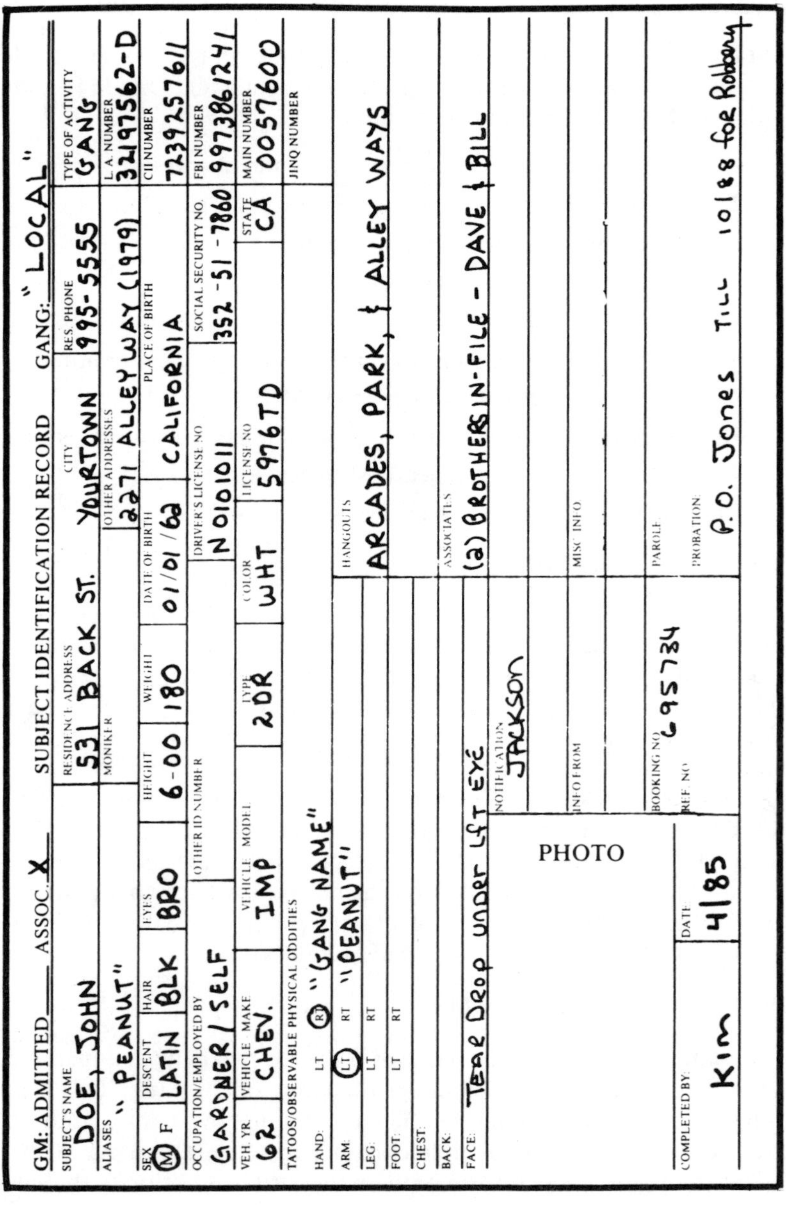

GM: ADMITTED____ ASSOC. X SUBJECT IDENTIFICATION RECORD GANG: "LOCAL"

SUBJECT'S NAME: DOE, JOHN
RESIDENCE ADDRESS: 531 BACK ST.
CITY: YOURTOWN
RES. PHONE: 995-5555
TYPE OF ACTIVITY: GANG
ALIASES: "PEANUT"
MONIKER:
OTHER ADDRESSES: 2271 ALLEY WAY (1979)
L. A. NUMBER: 32197562-D
SEX: (M) F
DESCENT: LATIN
HAIR: BLK
EYES: BRO
HEIGHT: 6-00
WEIGHT: 180
DATE OF BIRTH: 01/01/62
PLACE OF BIRTH: CALIFORNIA
CII NUMBER: 7239257611
OCCUPATION/EMPLOYED BY: GARDNER / SELF
OTHER ID NUMBER:
DRIVER'S LICENSE NO: N 0101011
SOCIAL SECURITY NO.: 352-51-7860
FBI NUMBER: 9973861241
VEH. YR.: 62
VEHICLE MAKE: CHEV.
VEHICLE MODEL: IMP
TYPE: 2DR
COLOR: WHT
LICENSE NO: 5976TD
STATE: CA
MAIN NUMBER: 0057600
TATOOS/OBSERVABLE PHYSICAL ODDITIES
JINQ NUMBER:
HAND: LT (RT) "GANG NAME"
ARM: (LT) RT "PEANUT"
LEG: LT RT
FOOT: LT RT
CHEST:
BACK:
FACE: TEAR DROP UNDER LFT EYE
HANGOUTS: ARCADES, PARK, & ALLEY WAYS
ASSOCIATES: (2) BROTHERS IN-FILE - DAVE & BILL
PHOTO
NOTIFICATION: JACKSON
INFO FROM:
MISC INFO:
BOOKING NO: 695734
REF. NO:
PAROLE:
COMPLETED BY: KIM
DATE: 4/85
PROBATION: P.O. Jones TILL 10/88 for Robbery

Figure 6.1 Sample gang member identification card (front).

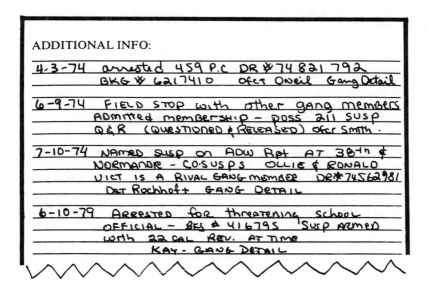

ADDITIONAL INFO:

4-3-74 arrested 459 P.C DR # 74 821 792
BKG # 621 7410 ofcr ONeil Gang Detail

6-9-74 FIELD STOP with other gang members
ADmitted membership - poss all susp
Q&R (QuesTiONeD & ReleAsed) ofcr Smith.

7-10-74 NAmeD SuSp on ADW Rpt AT 38th &
NORmANDie - CO·SuSPs OLLIe & RONALO
VicT IS A RivAL GANG member DR#74562981
DeT Rockhoft GANG DeTAiL

6-10-79 ARRESTeD for threatening school
OFFiciAL - BKs # 416795 'SuSp ARmeD
With 22 CAL Rev. AT TiMe
KAY - GANG DeTAiL

Figure 6.2 Sample gang member identification card (back).

The Moniker File

This file connects the subject's street name to his true identity and gang affiliation. In order to conserve space, it may be beneficial to combine several gang members who use the same moniker on one card. This procedure will also save time when searching the file (*See Figure 6.4*).

The Photograph File

Photographs, when available, are maintained on a gang member's identification card. Generally, when these photos are needed to conduct a show-up, two methods are used. One method is to remove the photo from the gang member's card and place it in a photo line-up folder for victims and witnesses to view. This procedure is followed most often when the number of possible suspects is limited.

Another method, used when there is a large number of possible gang suspects, is to use a "mug" or photo book. This book may be divided according to gang, with each photo identified by a code or number and cross-referenced to an alphabetical index of names in the front of the book. A precautionary word may be needed at this point: Many victims and witnesses are rival gang members, and the photos should not allow the identification of possible suspects by name.

The Gang Vehicle File

A gang vehicle file can be arranged in various patterns. This file consists of a card on each vehicle owned or used by identified gang members and associates. One workable method would be to have a description file arranged alphabetically according to the make of the vehicle, the year, license plate, number, color, body type, gang, owner, and other persons who may use the car. Having this information on hand makes it possible to conduct file searches when all that is known is the description of the car. The file can be made even more valuable by including information about the make of cars that members of different ethnic groups typically prefer, as well as the type of modification a particular group makes on its vehicles. This additional data can further facilitate gang vehicle identification.

Another workable method is to file vehicles alphabetically according to gang. This procedure reduces the number of vehicles to be checked, and in a short time a detective can check the vehicles of a gang. A shortcoming of this kind of file is evident. If it is not known which gangs operate within a jurisdiction, additional effort and exper-

GANG ACTIVITIES FILE

Figure 6.3 Sample gang member "pointer" file

tise will be required to investigate the possibilities, and this effort will usually be centered in a limited area. Because of the different circumstances involved, the type of system used must be tailored to fit the requirements of a particular law enforcement agency.

A vehicle file is a useful tool, but it does require constant attention. One final thought to keep in mind is that gang members often do not use their personal vehicles in planned raids or criminal activities because they can be recognized. However, since gang violence is frequently spontaneous in nature, known gang vehicles continually appear in crime reports. This tendency holds true especially for capers within a gang's turf or the turf of their rivals. Time permitting, gang members most often prefer to use stolen vehicles, as these are expendable and can be abandoned when no longer needed.

The following case best illustrates this point. One evening, two gang members walked into a party and discovered they were in the wrong neighborhood. They were forcibly ejected and escaped the rival gang with only minor injuries. Not to let the insult go without a challenge, they returned to their home-turf miles away, and shortly thereafter gathered seven additional gang members and two stolen cars. All the suspects returned to the rival area, near the location of the party. A gang member in one of the stolen cars rammed a rival's vehicle which was parked in front of the party. The noise of the impact caused the party-goers to come outside. The driver was then chased by some of the gang members from the party, around the corner to an awaiting

MONIKER:	"PEANUT"				
	NAME	D.O.B.	GANG	PUT INTO FILE BY:	DATE PUT INTO FILE
1	DOE, John	1-1-62	LOCAL	O'NEIL	1-82
2					
3					
4					
5					
6					
7					
8					
9					
10					

Figure 6.4 Sample gang member moniker file.

ambush. A stabbing occurred, and a rival gang member from the party was killed. The suspects fled in the other stolen car. Five of the seven suspects were arrested next day, in yet another stolen car (*See Figure 6.5*).

SECURITY AND ACCOUNTABILITY FOR FILES

The officer in charge of the gang investigative unit is responsible for the security of the files and is accountable for their contents. Although concern for the safety of the files in a physical sense is ever present,

Year	Vehicle Make	Color	License No.	Gang
1962	*Chev.*	*wht*	*5976 TD*	*Local*
Model		Vehicle Oddities		Gang Descent
IMP				*Latin*
Type				
2 DR				
				Date of Birth
	Driver	*DOE, John*		*1-1-62*
Date Veh. in File	Pass. in Veh 1			
1-82		2		
Put in File By		3		
O'NEIL	Reg. Owner			

Figure 6.5 Sample gang member vehicle file.

responsibilities for the data go further. In the first place, a balance has to be maintained between security and accessibility. Screened, trained personnel must be available to retrieve information for those authorized personnel who require it—and when they require it. But the problem that arises is that good files lose their value in direct proportion to the number of people who have physical access to them. These persons include not only those who need information and can retrieve it, but the personnel who update and purge the files as well. The officer in charge, needless to say, is going to have to walk a tight-rope, balancing the need to know against the need to maintain the integrity of the files.

Purging Files

Gang files should be re-examined on a regular basis to determine if the gangs included are still active and deserving of the time invested in maintaining the information. The formation and dissolution of gangs is fluid. If the files are not kept up-to-date they become distorted and lose their value. Continually adding gang members to an index expands the files to a point where they no longer represent an accurate picture of the gang. The files must show the active or potentially active gang member—not everyone who has ever been a member. If a person on file is identified as a gang member or associate member, and subsequently breaks away from the gang and is no longer involved with it, provisions must be made to remove his name from the files.

This purging must be done on a regular basis in order to maintain the integrity of the gang files and to ensure the protection of the individual's rights. The criteria for purging should be established and discussed with the agency's legal staff or advisors. The Los Angeles Police Department, for example, operates under the policy that on an ongoing basis, all subject identification cards having no entry relating to violent crimes or gang activity for the preceding two year period are purged from the files of their gang section. "Purge" means to get rid of or eliminate. It does not mean to refile in an inactive file or to relocate for future activation. If a gang unit is operating under legal restrictions in this matter, a lack of good faith—no matter how well-meaning the intentions—could jeopardize the balance of the unit's operation and existence.

Many officers and gang detectives state, however, that valuable information is lost when a file is purged in accordance with the the two-year, no-contact rule. They assert, and correctly so, that it is not uncommon for members of certain gangs to change chapters, as it were, and become active in another state for a few years—only to return to the old gang. In other cases, a gang member may have been in prison for a few years or confined to a youth facility, and thus, purged from the file. Then, upon his release from custody, he returns to his gang and picks up where he left off.

One way to counter this problem is to have the investigator assume the burden of showing clearly why the individual should not be purged from the gang files. One must also be able to document the reasons for retaining the card longer than two years.

Criteria should be established to keep the gang files current to a level where the information is of value, and the files are not burdened with members who are no longer involved in gang activity. The larger and more complex the gang files are, the more difficult they are to purge. The purging of one member from a file frequently involves purging that individual from several other, cross-referencing files, as well.

AUTOMATION OF GANG FILES

Many agencies have automated systems that with only slight modifications can retrieve information on a selective basis, an example of which is an automated field interview system. Using this system, a detective can determine which gang members from what gangs were stopped by a law enforcement agent, in what area the stop was made, at what time of day or night, and on what date. He can also quickly - find out whom the suspects were with, and if in a vehicle, its description. A check of monikers can yield additional information. Many systems have an added capacity to furnish data of this kind on printouts.

The value of the information, as with most records, depends on its source and subsequent interpretation. Each piece of information is only as reliable and valuable as the officer making the contact permits it to be. Since quality is an issue, the gang expert must evaluate not only the information, but its source. Among some of the questions to be kept in mind when evaluating data included in the system are the qualifications of the informant to determine whether a subject is a gang member, and whether the informant actually knows what he or she is talking about, or whether he or she is simply guessing and filling out boxes on a field interview form. Furthermore, experience has shown that it is probably unwise to identify a person as a gang member, based on a field interview or on the report of an officer who does not specialize in gang work. If a subject is placed in a file, the responsible officers or detectives must be ready, if need be, to explain the reasoning that led them to conclude that the individual so identified is actually a member of a gang.

An important thought that, it is hoped, will emerge is that files—and particularly the information in them—are not simply by-products of investigations. They should be units of information flexible enough to include the most important details of investigative efforts, yet stable and clear enough to ensure an accurate picture of the problems faced. Gangs thrive in an atmosphere of anonymity, and thoughtfully maintained gang files can remove that advantage.

CHAPTER 7

POLICE PATROL PROCEDURES

OFFICER'S RAPPORT

The authors would not presume to dictate patrol procedures to experienced line officers or departments. Established patrol procedures that meet individual departmental guidelines should be adhered to at all times. One purpose of this chapter is to assist line officers, by offering some proven methods of patrolling those areas influenced by street gangs.

A second purpose of this chapter is to emphasize that it is in the best interests of the patrol officer—and everybody in the community, as well—for him or her to relate as positively as possible with street gangs, without compromising the dignity and integrity of the badge one wears.

Because of the nature of their duties, uniformed officers will probably make more consistent contact with street gangs than any other law enforcement officer. The uniformed officer, during his or her daily shift, comes into contact with gangs by responding to calls concerning crimes, traffic stops, and checks of suspicious circumstances and/or persons.

These contacts may afford an officer an opportunity to understand and develop a rapport with the gang members and with the people who live in a *barrio* or ghetto. To do so could facilitate the job of the uniformed officer, and make the community somewhat safer. Rapport and common sense never got anyone killed.

Even though an officer may find a street gang offensive to his or her sense of decency, the simple fact of the matter is that there is nothing illegal per se in belonging to a gang. Street gangs are not going to disappear just because society finds them repulsive. Furthermore, experience and studies have yet to show an instance in which a street gang was dissolved or put out of action solely because of suppressive police action. When police pressure is intensified on a street gang, its members typically go underground and become secretive, which may produce even greater problems. Therefore, start easy when working with a street gang. The level of pressure can always be increased as the situation dictates.

Any confrontation involving a street gang has the potential to turn violent. Therefore, have a plan of action prepared beforehand. Such a plan contributes immeasurably in developing a pattern of police response that is rational, measured, and uniformly understandable. These plans, by necessity, must be flexible as well as consistent and will vary from community to community. No prepared comment in a textbook can cover all contingencies relative to working with these gangs. More will be said about the matter of violence in a few moments. However, the following suggestions are drawn from experience and are general enough that they may be some help to the officer on patrol.

For example, as officers cover their beat, they may observe gang members at their known hangout and feel duty bound to check for illegal activities. After taking prudent self-protection measures (i.e., calling the location, requesting back-up when appropriate, observing the scene before approaching it, etc.), and assuring themselves no crime has been committed, the officers might initiate a "rap" session. Several constructive things could be accomplished thereby. First, the officers let the gang know they are aware of its identity, thus removing the protective cloak of anonymity. That in itself is worth the time. Another advantage is that by stopping and rapping when a situation is calm, the officers establish themselves as persons who can be talked to—not just as adversaries who are seen only when there is trouble. The contact could also demonstrate that the officers are human beings who can, if given the chance, share the concerns, feelings, and thoughts of the gang. This contact could further serve as a humanizing process for all parties and might pay great dividends in the future.

THE REALITY OF VIOLENCE

Street gangs exist and function in the community from a base of strength gained through violent behavior. It would seem that a basic tenet of a gang is that its strength makes what ever it does "right." Therefore, a patrol officer must establish his or her authority in a way that gang members can relate to. That does not mean that officers become a law unto themselves or behave in any way that is less than professional or legal. However, officers can ill afford to show weakness in a face-to-face contact with a gang. If a gang feels it can intimidate an officer, the gang will destroy that officer's ability to work a beat. Thus the first role of a beat officer is to do what must be done: if arrests are to be made, make them; if citations are to be given, give them.

When a violent confrontation seems imminent, and all efforts have been made to avert it, act decisively. Request enough back-up units to do whatever is necessary. As stated before, gangs operate on the premise that their might makes them right. Therefore, be certain that you have what you need beforehand to get the job done. Violence is a way of life to gangs, and on some occasions it is simply a matter of preserving one's own life to respond in kind. The reponse the officer makes must always be definite and in accordance with department policy. (For complete details, see Rutledge, *The Officer Survival Manual,* Custom Publishing Company).

THE PARADOX

Paradoxically the gang typically will not retaliate against an individual patrol officer if it views the officer's actions as warranted and fair. There seems to be a perverted code of "ethics" within gangs that has evolved over a number of years. Though the code is unwritten, it is understood and accepted. While gangs do not necessarily approve of law enforcement action against them, there will seldom be retaliation if the action seems fair and warranted by the circumstances and within the law. However, if a gang feels it was treated "unfairly", the officer involved will be subject to almost constant confrontation and harassment. In a pathological way, it seems that a gang commits an act, passes judgement on itself, and then accepts punishment—as long as the punishment seems justified.

What is being suggested here is that when taking firm action, the action must be fair. The officer must at all times maintain a professional demeanor and act according to established department guidelines. Keep in mind that the police officer is probably the key authority figure with whom the gang member has dealt. As such, officers must themselves show their respect for the law by their behavior. The officer, whether he realizes it or not, is a *de facto* role model.

CONTROL OF GANG ACTIVITIES

Once an identifiable gang problem has surfaced, the officer on patrol can effectively undermine the gang's grip on a neighborhood by concentrating on certain aspects of the members' lifestyles. To accomplish this, emphasis must be placed on controlling the gang's overall activity.

The officer must become familiar not only with the members themselves but their daily routines. This may be effectively accomplished by the officer during the workday. He or she should maintain a close liaison with school officials, area businesses, and citizens within the area. Elementary school children are excellent sources of information, as they have generally not developed an animosity toward the police officer and will openly discuss neighborhood problems, such as the street gangs. Officers must make their first priority the identification of gang members operating within their area.

PERSONALITY IDENTIFICATION

Street gangs operate best from a position of anonymity. Their strength is drawn from the collective body of the gang, not the individual member's identity. The uniformed officer's first step in neutralizing the activity of the gang is to begin identifying the individuals in it. Learning not only the member's proper names but also his nickname, or moniker, sets the member apart from the faceless gang. He then becomes an individual who can be dealt with accordingly. Now that the officer knows this one individual, he or she should set about identifying the member's associates as they all, very likely, belong to the same clique or set within the gang.

After the identification process has begun, the officer should begin to observe the individual personalities of the gang members. It is surprisingly easy to identify those who are particularly violence-prone. It is these "hot heads" that are apt to be involved in the explosive violence for which street gangs are noted. These *vato locos* or "shooters" have the respect of their gangs, and identification of this group is of critical importance.

The officer should not make the mistake of thinking the members of this group of hot-blooded individuals are the only ones with whom to become familiar. In the background of the gang, many times obscured by the more flashy or exuberant members, awaits a personality that can be most dangerous. This person's attitude may be quiet and unassuming. He may initially appear to be only a peripheral member at best; but as the officer's inter-relation with the gang develops, the subtle strengths of this individual's influence on his fellow gang members will become more apparent. Other members will gravitate toward him; his advice will be sought on matters that are of concern to the gang as a whole. In short, this individual has all the charisma inherent to born leaders. His reactions will not necessarily be based on the emotions of the moment, but may be coolly planned and executed.

As discussed previously, few gangs have an identifiable leadership; that is the case even with this type of individual. He is likely to be only one of several persons with similar personalities within the gang, and he will exercise his control over those select few within his clique or set. It is for this reason that officers working a particular gang area must not limit their inquiry into personalities only to certain members, but must include each individual in the gang.

GANG HANGOUTS

The gang will, generally, have one or more favorite hangouts. The members will utilize these places to plan street crimes or attacks on rivals, and will retreat to them after executing the act. A thorough knowledge of these locations is of utmost importance to the beat officer, who should also make particular note of the escape routes to and from them. This information ensures that the deployment of containment forces can be accomplished quickly and completely if at some point a tactical police response is necessary.

DAILY OPERATIONS

Once field officers have familiarized themselves with the street gang and the diverse personalities in it, how should they conduct day-to-day patrol activities in relation to the gang? Knowing the gang is not enough; officers must maintain an awareness of community events that affect their ability to maintain order. One of the most important tactics officers have at their disposal is maintaining constant citizen contact. One must never allow that source of information to fade.

During the shift's patrol period, the absence of gang members at their favorite haunts or the lack of small children playing in open areas should immediately alert the officer that something is amiss in the neighborhood. It is at this time that the rapport previously developed with the citizens will yield the answers necessary to assist the officer in circumventing potential problems.

Being aware of the area's gang graffiti is another method for keeping track of gang activity. If, suddenly, unexplained cross-outs of the gang's graffiti occur, something within the gang has precipitated that. As the crossing-out is a challenge to the gang, one should expect serious, even violent events to follow, and prepare accordingly. This preparation should include gathering information through street contacts to identify the problem, exchanging information with other officers patrolling adjacent beats or shifts, and, if necessary, saturating the area with additional police units until the problem abates (*See Figure 7.1*).

FIELD INTERVIEWS

An additional tool the officer has at his or her disposal is the field interview report (F.I.R.). The importance of this simple report cannot be overstated. Maintaining daily contact with the gang and logging this activity put the gang on notice that its activities are being scrutinized.

Another tactic that has proven effective on the gang member, especially psychologically, is to tell him exactly why the F.I.R. is being prepared. This suggests to him that he could be connected to any criminal conduct in the area, and many times curtails his activity for a period of time. The officer that consistently utilizes F.I.R.'s will

Figure 7.1 Depicts crossed out gang graffiti.

notice that his or her knowledge of the gang and intra-gang relationships is enhanced greatly.

Another side benefit of field interviews is the breaking down of imperceptible barriers between the officer and the gang member. When asked by the officer if he belongs to the neighborhood gang, the gang member is very likely to admit membership. If at a later date it becomes legally necessary to prove the individual's gang affiliation, it will be simply a matter of showing the F.I.R. as evidence. The self-admission is of significant value in that the officer has not attached a damaging label to the youth, but by his own admission the gang member has done so himself.

OFFICER'S ROLE

Officers must not base their judgment of an individual solely on vague impressions without the benefit of careful inquiries. Setting aside the legal question, the contact and interreaction allow an opportunity for the lowering of those barriers that exist and for establishing a dialogue.

Finally, it is most important to remember that the beat officer is in a position to be the most knowledgeable and important source of information available to investigators on local conditions within the area. The relationship established by an officer with the citizens on his or her beat is the key to effectiveness.

The positive deportment of the uniformed officer, along with personal knowledge of the area and local gangs, may be the most effective deterrent to gang activity in today's society. Many times it is due solely to the officer's action that a gang learns that criminal behavior will not be tolerated.

CHAPTER 8

TECHNIQUES OF GANG INVESTIGATIONS

UNIQUENESS OF GANG CRIME

Gang members are involved in a wide variety of criminal activities. Many of these crimes are spontaneous and range from minor acts of vandalism to murder. Most street gang murders are not executions perpetrated by a highly organized, sophisticated gang, as is often portrayed in the movies. They are committed by emotional, violent gang members who do not think of the consequences. Therefore, a gang investigation is unique, not because of the crime being investigated, but because of the fact that gang members are involved. Whatever it is that sets the guilty member apart from the others (whether it be attitude, philosophy, group pressure or some other factor), it is this difference that holds the key to the solving of the crime.

This chapter is not intended as a course in either basic or advanced criminal investigation. Rather, it is designed to offer additional investigative tools, thus providing a headstart and a direction. To do this, we will cover various facets of gang investigation ranging from the collection of background information essential to a gang investigator, following through to the crime scene, and concluding with the identification and arrest of the suspects. As you will see, a great deal of this material will be quite familiar to the experienced investigator. However, in the excitement and confusion of an investigation much can be overlooked, even by experienced detectives.

PREPARATION

A detective does not have to be a gang expert to solve a gang-related crime. Most cases can be solved by applying standard investigative techniques and procedures. Nonetheless, detectives experienced in gang activity are able to identify or eliminate possible suspects and supply investigative insights and background information. Hours of investigative "wheel spinning," chasing fictitious leads are reduced when the detectives know the gangs involved. The officer charged with the responsibility of a gang-involved investigation should be prepared to ask and answer the following questions:

1. Which gangs are active in the jurisdiction and what are their individual boundaries?
2. Who are the members of each gang and are they hard-core or associate members (both are important and may assume different roles)?
3. Are the monikers or street names of the different members matched with their true identities?
4. Which gangs are fighting and with whom? Is there an ongoing war?
5. Does the crime fit a specific pattern of a particular gang?

The answers to these questions can best be supplied by personnel assigned to a gang unit. If gang specialists are not available and the assigned detective lacks background on the gangs involved, there are other sources of information. Juvenile and uniformed officers, especially those that patrol school areas, are generally well aware of local gang activity.

Also, keep in mind that in every police organization there are officers who, in addition to their assigned activity, concentrate attention on a certain type of criminal. Many are concerned with "hype" burglars and develop a personal expertise and their own files on these suspects. Other officers follow similar procedures with gang members. These files, compiled by interested, individual officers, have positive and negative features—but most often the information is current and will prove useful. However, the information must be available. The following hypothetical account illustrates the problem.

A detective is assigned to investigate a gang crime and needs additional information. An officer working a patrol assignment has developed personal expertise and a file on gang members within an area of assignment. The officer, in all probability, knows who the suspects are and where they can be located. Certainly personal files could offer investigative leads. As luck would have it, the officer is on vacation and cannot be reached. His file is either locked and hidden somewhere or it is with him. Consequently, the detective is not able to utilize the information. Is the officer being selfish or unthinking by taking the file with him? Perhaps, but there may be other considerations. Of course, we know what could happen to the file if the officer did not hide it and it was readily available to everyone. It is a problem of control and responsibility. The officer takes pride in his efforts and strives to maintain the files in the best-possible condition, but unfortunately, there are others who lack the same degree of care and attention to detail. Thus photos and other items of information may be taken from the file to be used in the investigation and for various reasons not returned. Time after time this seems to happen and the files soon lose their value. Consequently, the officer locks them away to preserve the information. The result is either information that is incomplete (as in the case of files that are picked over and not monitored), or information is unavailable in the absence of the officer.

All expertise, information, and assistance is worthless if it is not available when it is needed. This is true for a one-man file or a unit of gang experts. The key to information is availability. The final consideration about the use of unofficial files is their legality. These personal files must meet the same standards and legal requirements adhered to by the agency. If not, the results of any suspect identification risks being suppressed in court.

FIELD INTERVIEW SYSTEM

It must be stressed that a detective does not need a large gang unit to obtain the information needed to solve a gang crime. A good field interview system is a valuable tool. This is especially true if the cards include, in addition to the standard information, specific items pertaining to gang activity. For example, there should be spaces set aside to show if the subject belongs to a gang and what the name of the gang is. Another space should indicate if the interview was conducted as a result of gang activity.

The spaces allotted for monikers, tattoos, associates, and vehicles are critically important in gang investigations. Frequently, the only lead, along with the name of the involved gang, is the street name or moniker of the suspect. The field interview card can identify the suspect by his true name and show that he uses a particular moniker.

This brings us to another identifier: tattoos. The interview card must not only indicate that the person has tattoos, but describe what they are and where they are located. Nothing is more frustrating than to be searching for a suspect with a particular tattoo, only to find that the portion of the card listing tattoos indicates "yes" or "numerous" instead of a specific description.

Vehicle information should be as complete as possible and include any unusual features. If the vehicle has a plaque or inscription naming a van or car club, it should be noted. Associates are also important and must be cross-referenced, allowing the detective to link all the subjects together.

CRIME SCENE CONSIDERATIONS

Crime scenes that involve gangs present elements that are unique. As a result, not only must sound investigative techniques be followed, but investigators must be especially careful not to restrict or limit the area of the crime scene. Therefore, the nature of such crimes, coupled with gang tactics, makes it essential to view the crime scene, not as an isolated environment, but as a part of a chain of events. For example, a common gang assault involves not only an attack but frequently a chase: either the suspects chasing the victims, or the victims' associates chasing the suspects. As a result, the crime scene may cover a wide area involving gunshot exchanges and chases over several square miles. More often than not, these battles end in traffic accidents that add to the confusion of the investigation.

The Expanded Area

For example, an expanded crime scene occurred in a war between two Los Angeles gangs which accounted for sixteen violent incidents in a short period of time. The crimes included ten drive-by shootings, three attempted murders, and three actual murders. This particular incident started when members of one gang drove into the neighborhood of a rival group and fired shotgun blasts at the house of a gang member. The attacking gang deliberately identified itself. A short time later, the rival gang attempted to return the "favor" and planned a retaliation raid. Two gang members drove to a location near the house used as a meeting place of the first gang. The driver of the car parked in a secluded location a block away and was to wait for his crime partner to return.

In the meantime, his colleague approached the house on foot and fired his .22 caliber revolver into the doors and windows until his gun was empty. As he tried to flee, he was ambushed by eight heavily armed rival gang members. Gunfire erupted and the chase was on. After a few blocks, the pursuing gang members had to return to the house for more ammunition. The fleeing gang member, now wounded by the barrage of bullets, discovered his driver had abandoned him, leaving him alone and on foot. He crawled under a parked car to hide, but was quickly found, pulled from his hiding place, and shot. His dying words were, "Kill me!!"

First appearances indicated a limited crime scene, and a three-house area was closed off pending the arrival of homicide detectives. Subsequent information disclosed the true size of the crime scene, but not before police officers and press personnel complicated the investigation by inadvertently trampling evidence. Thus, it cannot be overemphasized that the extent of a gang-related crime scene may be greater than it appears at first glance, and an investigator must withold final judgment until it can be determined what took place and where.

The Immediate Area

After determining the size of the crime scene, a gang investigator should take a close look at the area itself. That is, the investigator must try to find out which gang controls the area and how strong its control is. Is the crime scene in the middle of a one-gang housing project, or is it in an area open to many gangs? Were the suspects on foot or in a car? A car can speed through the heart of a rival gang area, but if the suspects had to have been on foot, then another dimension is added.

For example, in a homicide scene in a "one-gang" project area where the suspect had to approach the crime scene on foot, the investigator has to determine whether or not this was a commando-type raid by a rival gang, which would be quite rare. Gang members do not like to be on foot in a strange area, especially one dominated by their enemy. The odds are good that the suspects in the above instance are local and are possibly members of the same gang as the victim. These crimes generally reflect intra-gang conflicts involving narcotics, girlfriends, or family disputes. Therefore, the best starting point is with the members of the gang in control of the area.

Crime Scene Graffiti

Reading and understanding gang graffiti near a crime scene may assist the investigator, and important evidence may be unearthed by asking a few simple questions. For instance, if wall writings are present at the scene, the investigator should find out if the writings are old or new. If the writings are new, they may be linked to the crime. The victim may have been attacked while writing the graffiti; or, on the other hand, the attackers may have left the writings as an insult or challenge to the victim's gang. In either case, the importance of the graffiti must not be depreciated because the function of graffiti is not only to identify and delimit turf; but also, as stated elsewhere in this work, to establish identity. By defiling the gang's graffiti (thus, by extension, the member's identity), the attacking gang has presented an insult to which the defending gang must respond or lose face. The response will be violent and carried out without concern for human cost or consequences (*See Figures 8.1 and 8.2*).

VICTIMS AND WITNESSES

Scrutinizing and interviewing victims is also crucially important because the individuals who are being interviewed could be gang members involved in the crime and not just passive, innocent bystanders. Because of that, the investigator should first determine if any of the victims or witnesses have obvious tattoos. If so, the investigator should attempt to look at them closely, when possible, because tattoos reveal gang affiliations and nicknames or monikers which can lead to establishing a suspect's true identity. A victim's or witness' mode of dress is also important. If an individual is "dressed out" in gang style, then the style may lead to the identity of the gang or gangs involved. Another consideration regarding clothing has to do with suspects *not* dressed in gang style but in something suitable for a party. If so, then check for a party near the crime scene or in a nearby rival gang area. Suspects have used parties, weddings, funerals and wakes to build their courage for a retaliation and then returned to the gathering for an alibi. A wake or funeral for a gang member killed by a rival gang, for example, is a very emotional and potentially violent situation.

The location may be the scene of a "drive-by" shooting or attack by the rival gang attempting to disrupt the funeral. It is not uncommon for gang members, while attending a wake, to plan a retaliation and to leave and search for rival gang members to kill to "even the score." One such incident did happen when four carloads of gang members left a funeral home while services were in progress for a fellow

Figure 8.1 An example of "new" graffiti found at a homicide crime scene.

member. They drove into the rival gang area nearby, where they beat, stabbed, and then shot to death a suspected rival gang member. The suspects returned to the funeral. The victim was not a gang member, but was merely sitting on a bus bench. The suspects were observed returning to the funeral home and were subsequently arrested.

Verbal Exchanges And Challenges

Since gang crimes almost always include a verbal exchange between suspects and victims, it is important to try to learn what was said. In their swaggering way, gang members want to be sure the victim knows who is attacking him, or at least what gang, so some of the more brazen attackers even call out their own personal monikers to taunt the victim further.

The foregoing is especially true for a traditional Hispanic gang. Black gang members, in addition to calling out their gang's name during an attack—such as "Crip here"—may also use various hand signs to identify their gang. In incidents of gang versus gang attacks, the victims will know the attacking gang, although they may not choose to reveal such information to the police.

Figure 8.2 An example of recently crossed out graffiti found at a crime scene.

Physical Evidence

Physical evidence is a constant factor regardless of gang involvement, and standard investigative procedures apply. With gang crimes, the chances are greater that the victims and witnesses are not just passive bystanders. In fact, such individuals are often involved as aggressors and victims, enjoying mutual combat. Allowing for this fact, evidence at the crime scene becomes increasingly important.

Evidence may be hidden or destroyed by the victim or witnesses in an effort to shift suspicion away from them. It is a sound practice for investigators, then, to search for weapons hidden near the crime scene. However, if time permits, the combatants themselves will remove any evidence from the scene before the police arrive.

WITNESS SECURITY

Obviously, gang members are generally very unreliable as witnesses. Consequently, it is important to find a witness who is not a gang member. In gang cases, this is usually difficult, especially immediately after a crime. Non-gang witnesses are reluctant to come forward to offer information to the authorities. An investigator may have to return to the scene after the excitement settles. To say the least, discretion is best when contacting potential witnesses; and when they are found, care must be taken not to jeopardize their safety unnecessarily.

For example, a detective decides to conduct a house-to-house interview operation covering a two-block area around a crime scene. The goal of the operation is to gather information about the crime and to locate additional witnesses. On the third interview, a witness is discovered and an initial statement is taken. The detective should continue and complete the rest of the interviews, if possible, for the following reasons.

First, if the police immediately leave the witness' house and go charging off to arrest the suspects in a flurry of screeching tires and flashing lights, the witness will be compromised. Within minutes, even if the suspect lives in another area, word has passed through the neighborhood, and the gang knows the witness' identity. Additional pressure can be avoided or delayed if the detective takes the necessary precautions to protect the witness' identity.

Second, the interviews should continue because an additional or even better witness may be found. Granted, some information must be acted on at once to ensure a quick apprehension. However, measures should be taken to secure the safety of the witness, or he will soon become uncooperative and "lose his memory." A note at this point about crime scene and field interviews: Witnesses in gang crimes are understandably often fearful and hesitant. The police must be aware of the possibility of gang intimidation. Tape recording the interview reduces the problems later in the investigation, and many police agencies, as standard procedure, use pocket or briefcase recorders in these situations.

Again, many witnesses to violent gang crimes are not impartial, but in some way tied to one of the gangs involved. If the victim and witnesses are gang members, the following information may normally be assumed. First, the victims know or suspect the identity of their assailants and their *placas* or monikers (i.e., gang street names). Next, they will probably know why the attack was made and where to find the suspects. Finally, they will very likely refuse to cooperate, opting for retaliation. When the identity of the attacking gang is not known for certain and needs to be confirmed, members of the victim's gang may attempt to get the information from the police by posing as disinterested third-party witnesses. Thus, while at the station, it is important to keep all witnesses apart until they can be interviewed.

Once the interviews begin, the investigator must consider whether or not his "witness" is not in reality a suspect in disguise. Other problems also emerge at this point: "witnesses" may lie in order to throw the investigator off the trail. It may be that the body of a murdered rival gang member was taken from the scene of his killing and placed elsewhere to confuse the issue. Witnesses may lie to cover up accidental shootings—the reasons and answers for which mean trouble with the law—so as a result, witnesses manufacture a story to protect themselves.

Sometimes the story is that the victim was injured in a drive-by shooting. This story is intended not only to cover up their own trail, but to cause a little difficulty for a rival gang. However, the description of the alleged attackers and their vehicle will usually be vague. Then as the investigators examine a wound, checking for powder residue and by threatening a trace-metal gun test, the lie begins to unravel quickly and the truth emerges.

Usually at this point in the investigation, enough information has been gathered to identify the suspects or at least the involved gang. The process of elimination then comes into play. First, by determining that the suspects are gang members, those who are not gang members can be eliminated from the list of suspects. Next, when the gang is known, still other possible suspects are eliminated. The investigator can see that in gang cases, he is dealing with a fixed cast of characters, most of them already known by the police. The next step is to target-in on the specific suspect.

SHOW-UPS

One of the best ways to connect a suspect to a crime is with a willing eyewitness. If the witness knows the suspect, the identification problem is simplified. However, in many gang crimes, the witness and the suspects are strangers, and the identification is accomplished through a show-up procedure. A show-up is simply a process of showing a witness a likeness of a suspect, as in a photograph or drawing. The two types of show-up used most frequently in gang cases are the witness and suspect confrontation (commonly referred to as the field show-up) and the photo show-up. A field show-up is good to use whenever possible and should be sought soon after the incident. It offers a witness an opportunity to make an identification while the circumstances are fresh in his mind. This type of show-up usually results from a quick police response that nets the possible suspects in the area of the crime scene. Officers are legally permitted to detain suspects only as long as it takes to determine their involvement in a crime. Thus, the witness should be brought to the suspects' location, unless circumstances justify transporting the suspect to the witness.

USE OF PHOTOS

Often times, suspects escape from the area of the crime. In that case, if an identification can be made at all, it will likely be through the use of photographs. The type of photo show-up will depend on the information the witness offers. For instance, if a witness says that he had never seen the suspects before the crime but would be able to identify them if he saw them again, and the investigator decides the suspects are probably gang members, a general showing of all photos in a gang mug book would be appropriate. As the number of suspects is narrowed down, then a limited show-up is used in which a photo of an individual suspect is displayed along with others as explained below.

Each witness, before seeing any photographs, must be admonished individually that a suspect's picture in a book does not necessarily mean that the subject is guilty of any crime. The wording of the admonishment can be printed on a show-up card or folder. Many police agencies use a printed form in both English and Spanish similar to the ones below.

PHOTOGRAPHIC LINEUP ADMONITION

In a moment I am going to show you a group of photographs. This group of photographs may or may not contain a picture of the person who committed the crime now being investigated. The fact that the photos are being shown to you should not cause you to believe or guess that the guilty person has been caught. You do not have to identify anyone. It is just as important to free innocent persons from suspicion as it is to identify those who are guilty. Please keep in mind that hairstyles, beards, and mustaches are easily changed. Also, photographs do not always depict the true complexion of a person—it may be lighter or darker than shown in the photo. You should pay no attention to any markings or numbers that may appear on the photos. Also, pay no attention to whether the photos are in color or black and white or any other difference in the type of style of the photographs. You should study only the person shown in each photograph. Please, do not talk to anyone other than police officers while viewing the photos. You must make up your own mind and not be influenced by other witnesses, if any. When you have completed viewing all the photos, please tell me whether or not you can make an identification. If you can, tell me, in your own words, how sure your are of your identification. Please do not indicate in any way to other witnesses that you have or have not made an identification.

PHOTOGRAPHIC LINEUP ADMONITION (SPANISH)

En un momento le voy a mostrar un grupo de fotografías. Este grupo de fotografías puede o no puede contener la imagen de la person que cometio el crimen que en estos monentos se está investigando. El hecho que las fotografías se muestran a Ud. no debe hacerlo creer o adivinar que la persona culpable ha sido arrestada. No está obligado a identificar persona alguna. Es tan importante libertar a personas inocentes de sospechas como lo es indentificar a los culpables. Por favor tenga en cuenta que estilos de la cabellera, barba y bigotes pueden cambiarse facilmente. También, fotografías no muestran siempre el color de la piel verdadero de una persona-podría ser más claro o mas obscuro de lo que se ve en la fotografía. No debe Ud. prestar atención alguna a marcas o números que aparezcan sobre las fotografías. Tampoco preste atención si las fotos son en colores o en blanco y negro o si existe cualquier otra diferencia de tipo o estilo entre las fotografías. Solamente debe estudiar la persona que se ve en cada fotografía. Sírvase no hablar con nadie que no sean oficiles de policia mientras Ud. esta estudiando las fotografías. Ud. debe hacer su propia decisión y no debe ser influenciado por otros testigos si los hubiere. Al haber terminado de mirar todas las fotografías, sírvase decirme si Ud. puede o no puede hacer una identificación. Por favor, no indique en forma alguna a otros testigos si Ud. ha hecho o no ha hecho una identificación.

Police investigators then generally have the witness sign the admonition portion of the show-up card.

Guidelines should be established and followed to be sure that the show-up procedure meets legal requirements. For each limited show-up (see above), the suspect's photo should be placed within a group which includes the photographs of six other individuals. These photos are matched so that no particular photo stands out. If the photo shows a suspect wearing a hat, mustache or beard, then the other photos should be of a like nature. It is not necessary that all of the photos be of gang members, but if they are, the number of photos of probable suspects should be limited to one or two per card.

Gang members commit crimes in groups, and these groups comprise their close associates. If a suspected gang member's photo is placed on a card with five of his associates and the crime is one involving multiple suspects, then a multiple identification may result. These types of identifications cause prosecution problems and raise doubt as to the validity of the photo show-up procedure and the witness' identification. Witnesses or victims viewing the photographs should be kept separated to avoid their influencing one another prior to making an identification.

If an identification is made, the witness should indicate which photo he identified. It is also good practice in cases in which there are multiple suspects to have the witness briefly describe the identified suspect's role in the crime. For example, the witness may write on the card: Photo No. 2 is a picture of the suspect that shot at me (the witness). After the witness signs his name, the officer or investigator should also sign and add the date, time, and location of the viewing. The investigator should keep in mind that the show-up folder and all of the photos will be used in court and may be admitted into evidence in a future trial.

OTHER SOURCES OF INFORMATION

Witnesses cannot always be found, so alternative investigative means should be explored. J. Edgar Hoover wrote in the *Law Enforcement Bulletin* in 1955, in part, that experience demonstrates that the cooperation of informants who can readily furnish accurate information is essential in criminal investigations. This is especially true in gang cases. Society seems to hold the term *informer* in a relatively negative light, frequently linking informers with organized crime or picturing them as corrupt, contemptible creatures hiding in the night.

This is not necessarily an accurate portrayal, because any person who is a source of information could be labeled an informer, but because of the pejorative connotation of the word, an investigator must use good judgment when using the term so as not to alienate potential sources of intelligence. In fact, most of the information police agencies receive about gangs comes from law-abiding citizens. Several of these sources will be briefly mentioned below.

First, it is expected that hard-core gang members seldom cooperate. They do not willingly offer leads or information, especially concerning their own gang. But often, they do try to impress their fellow members by being hostile to the questioning, or they may be afraid of reprisals for being a *rata* or "snitch." Yet, almost regardless of the seriousness of the crime, a gang member cannot seem to keep quiet about his gang exploits. In a very short time, his associates and even non-gang youths hear of the crime either from the suspect or through the grapevine. Suspects brag about the incident, and this bragging is used to build their reputation within the gang.

It is not surprising, therefore, that the Monday after a weekend gang shooting, the local school kids often know more about the case than the police. At times, their information, although usually exaggerated, will contain enough truth to lead investigators to the right suspects. For this reason, it is important for the police to maintain rapport with school personnel, security officers, teachers, and administrators. Many non-gang or pre-gang youth in the neighborhood like to talk to police officers and may have current information about a recent crime or a knowledge of the events which served as a background for the crime.

Another source of information is park and recreation employees. They are aware of the gang activity in their assigned park and who the more active members are. The local youngsters will usually come to park employees with rumors of gang activity before they will tell the police. Bear in mind that park directors may have established rapport with a gang and will be hesitant or avoid outright talking to the police when gang members are present. However, such employees may later privately phone in needed information. This pattern may also hold true for members of the clergy in the neighborhood, small-business people, long-time residents, and postal employees. Using these people and the other numerous sources of information, the police will eventually identify the suspect. In fact, the identification of suspects involved in gang crimes is not necessarily the most difficult task of the police.

LOCATING THE SUSPECTS

The next concern after identifying the suspect, of course, is to find him. This should be accomplished as soon as possible, especially in cases of serious and violent crimes. The fact that the suspect is a gang member actually aids in his capture because many aspects of gang behavior are predictable. For example, most gang crimes are not "hits" from professional assassins. Normally, a gang member does not shoot a rival and flee the country. Suspects that do flee the state or country will generally stay with relatives and eventually return to their home turf and their gang. Their family and gang are the most important things in their lives.

Gang members often do not think about the consequences of their acts in terms of capture or punishment, and those that do, may not change their objectives. An older and wiser gang member may not become directly involved in a crime, but may remain in an advisory role. The younger members are often used by the gang for everything from carrying messages or narcotics to committing robberies or murders. From the viewpoint of the gang, the younger the member, the better: if he is caught, the criminal justice system is usually not severe with him because of his youth.

Regardless of the success or failure of the youth's attack, he gains precious (to him) gang recognition. He has proven his loyalty. It does not matter if he escapes capture or is arrested, convicted, and sent to camp. He still gains status within the gang—to the young gang member seeking acceptance, it seems he cannot lose.

Police officers are generally aware of the strong ties that exist between a gang member and his turf. Therefore, gang hangouts and "crash pads" should be among the first places to check for wanted members. It is to these places that a member goes to recount his exploits, build his prestige, and develop an alibi. It is also common for gang members to change locations daily (this practice is known as "sleeping around"). The suspect in such situations is harbored by older gang members who encourage and, thus, indirectly assist the younger ones to commit crimes.

One way of dealing with the older members who are recalcitrant and refuse to assist the authorities in finding a suspect is to remind uncooperative individuals of the Principals and Accessory Section of the Penal Code. Simply stated, anyone who helps a suspect to avoid arrest in any way is guilty of a crime. Such reminders generally are very helpful in getting wanted information, in that older gang members typically do not want to return to prison, especially for a crime they were not originally involved in.

Knowing and using these sections can increase pressure to obtain wanted information. The investigator will encounter a number of other gang members during the search, and depending on the circumstances of the investigation, he or she may decide to inform these members that the suspect is wanted for a felony. The investigator would not be telling the gang members anything they probably did not already know. The investigator should further explain enough of the Principal and Accessory Section to be sure that the person being addressed understands that if he conceals or aids a suspect, he may be arrested as an accessory to a felony. This admonition, too, should be written down or documented and signed by witnesses. And if a suspect is captured at the home of one who has been admonished, there may be additional arrests. This second arrest is more important than it appears at first sight because it works to break down the cohesiveness of the gang.

Other likely locations to find wanted gang members include the suspect's home, his parents' home, a girlfriend's house, or the home of some other close relative. Many investigators talk with relatives or friends to have them persuade the individual to turn himself in. This move can save family and friends from the danger of a gang retaliation strike in which they would be innocent bystanders and also remove the suspect from a dangerous confrontation with the police when he is eventually arrested.

Realizing the hopelessness of continued flight and the danger in which they are placing themselves, their families and friends, many gang members give themselves up to the authorities. It is in everyone's best interest, therefore, to keep the pressure on when searching for a suspect. To do so will very often help to avert further bloodshed and killings.

WARRANTS

A warrant in its simplest terms is an order by a judge or magistrate directing the police to arrest a particular individual or to search a specific location for certain items of evidence. A warrant can enter the investigative process at various levels and its success depends on current and accurate information. The adage of seeking a warrant soon after a crime is especially valid in gang investigations because the longer the delay in beginning the warrant process, the more difficult the task becomes. Information that is "stale" or "old" generally is of little value in securing a warrant.

A search warrant for weapons used in a gang-related crime should authorize a search for ammunition as well as for the weapon. This is because the kind of ammunition used can be good evidence, especially if the weapon being sought, for example, is an automatic. In these cases, the possibility exists that the suspects "raked" ammunition through the gun while checking the action, and each weapon, of course, leaves its characteristic mark on the bullets. Not infrequently, bullets may be matched with casings left at the crime scene.

Search warrants should indicate that gun cleaning kits, receipts for ammunition purchases, and firearms ownership slips can also be taken as evidence. Such pieces of evidence taken into custody in one homicide investigation turned out to be crucial. In this instance, a suspect in a gang fight used a sawed-off shotgun to blast his opponent. Police officers armed with a search warrant entered the suspect's house and recovered the gun, the portion of the barrel that had been cut off, ammunition, and a bill of sale dated the previous day for both the gun and the ammunition. The acquisition of this evidence ruled out the suspect's contention that the shooting was a spontaneous act, and he was subsequently convicted of premeditated murder.

Other important evidence recovered during a search can link a suspect to a street gang, thereby establishing a strong motive for a crime. This type of evidence, often found in a gang member's bedroom, includes photos of the subject with other gang members, holding guns, "flashing" gang hand signs, holding a gang banner—sometimes even the bedroom walls themselves which have been decorated with graffiti and monikers of close associates. While it is impractical to take the wall to the courtroom, a good set of photographs will be worthwhile in future court proceedings. When the suspects during the trial deny gang membership, and many will, the prosecutor can make excellent use of the photos.

Search warrants not only help the officer gather specific evidence connecting a suspect to a crime, but may result in the recovery of many stolen guns. Taking weapons away from a gang diminishes the potential for violence, and even if only for a short period of time, it is worth the effort. Thus, search warrants judiciously applied are valuable tools that law enforcement can use to combat gang violence.

CASE PREPARATION

The identification and arrest of a gang member is not necessarily the most difficult aspect of a gang investigation. As discussed earlier, gang members feel a great bond to their turf, their gang, and at times, seem to have a pathological need to boast of their crimes. These facts, coupled with established and proven investigative techniques, permit the identification and apprehension of the gang member. Street gang crimes, and especially gang-involved homicides, continually show a high clearance rate. Clearing a crime means the authorities know who did it and have enough evidence to file a misdemeanor or felony complaint. The suspect may or may not be in custody.

The task of the investigator, particularly the gang investigator, is far from complete, however. The preparation of a case for a prosecution that will culminate in the conviction of the suspect may be the most critical portion of the entire investigation. The key to a successful prosecution lies in the preparation of the case. The investigator must take all of the facts and information gathered, along with supportive evidence, and present them to the prosecuting agency. The investigation at this point should be complete, leaving no unanswered questions. Rules of evidence, search, seizure and arrest procedures must have been followed in accordance with the law. The conclusions drawn from the investigation must be substantiated by provable evidence. (For complete details see: Rutledge, *The Search and Seizure Handbook for Law Officers,* Custom Publishing Company).

PRELIMINARY REPORTS

Frequently, an essential element in the investigation is the initial police report. Many non-homicide, gang-involved crime reports are completed by patrol officers. These reports must be accurate and contain as much detail as necessary to establish the elements of an alleged crime. If an arrest report is included, it must also show clearly the probable cause that led to the arrest of the suspect. Probable cause explains on what reasonable, legal grounds the officers proceeded as they did in investigating and in preparing to arrest a suspect. This report describes the information, observations, background and experience which led the officers to their conclusions and actions. Therefore, such reports—written by patrol officers—are a crucial element of the investigation. This is not to say that the reports of patrol officers are any more important than those of their investigative counterparts. However, when omissions and errors in a case come to light, this report is one of the first documents scrutinized. Sometimes the investigator is required to use his own background and experience to interpret the discussion of the probable cause hidden between the words and sentences of a report. The prosecutor and the court may not have either the experience or the time to do so. Consequently, it is the responsibility of the investigator to clarify each point before it goes to the prosecutor. If the report is incomplete, the case will not be filed and the suspect will go free. (See: Rutledge, *The New Police Report Manual,* Custom Publishing Company).

PROSECUTION STRATEGY

Throughout the investigation the detective should think in terms of prosecution. Doing so reduces the chances of surprise questions raised by the defense during the trial that would destroy the prosecution's case. The sooner uncertain issues are settled, the less opportunity the suspect's associates have to intimidate witnesses and fabricate an alibi for their fellow gang member. Furthermore, all witnesses and suspects should be locked into an account of the incident. Usually, this is accomplished by taking written or tape-recorded statements.

Next, the detective should anticipate tactics by the defense and be able to counter them quickly. All alibis must be checked as soon as possible to clear the innocent or to catch the suspect in a lie. When the suspect's guilt appears obvious, defense attorneys may choose a different strategy.

DEFENSE STRATEGY

The two most often used defense strategies are pleas of diminished capacity and self-defense. If the prosecution is surprised by these ploys and cannot counter effectively, it may very likely lose the case. For example, if a suspect is arrested for murder and it seems he may be under the influence of drugs, alcohol, or both, a narcotics expert and a medical doctor can be of assistance in determining the extent or degree, if any, of intoxication and thus, of diminished capacity. (Note: Diminished capacity has been eliminated as a defense in some states). Additionally, the interviewing officer or investigator will also form an opinion relative to the suspect's mental capacity to make an informed judgement. This opinion—based on the suspect's behavior, demeanor, and answers to questions—may be useful during the trial. The time at which the suspect was tested for drugs or alcohol is important because it may establish whether the suspect was under the influence before or after the crime took place. This consideration, obviously, is fundamental to a successful plea of diminished capacity or lack of intent due to drugs or alcohol.

Another defense maneuver used in gang-related murder cases is a plea of self-defense. One such case involved members of two rival gangs who were attending a community dance. A minor altercation broke out, after which one gang member left. He returned with an eight-inch hunting knife—then stabbed the victim repeatedly. During the trial the accused claimed he was acting in self-defense against an armed attacker. After a careful, detailed investigation, a witness gave pertinent information which caused the collapse of the claim of self-defense.

Therefore, it is important to be able to detail the events surrounding a crime and to account for the actions of suspects and victims. However, this is often difficult because the involved parties offer statements that are either self-serving or designed to shift blame to their adversary. Independent, non-involved witnesses are the best source of the truth, but such witnesses are difficult to find and even more difficult to keep. (See Rutledge, *Courtroom Survival, The Officer's Guide to Better Testimony,* Custom Publishing Company).

WITNESS INTIMIDATION

Witness intimidation has destroyed more cases than anyone wants to admit. The witness is concerned not only with his or her safety, but the well-being of loved ones. How should this problem be approached? Investigators should be honest in their dealings with all witnesses, especially those who are fearful. Nothing should be promised, for any reason, that cannot be delivered. The Hard-Core Gang Section of the District Attoney's Office for the County of Los Angeles encounters witness intimidation cases daily. The unit deals with each situation on a one-by-one basis because there is no organized plan or program that addresses the issues encountered when witnesses are subjected to violence or threats of violence. It seems that when the problem arises, each agency involved defers jurisdiction to the others. On the other hand, many agencies work closely with the prosecutors to ensure witness protection. The Hard-Core Gang Section's experience and success point up the need for witness protection not only in violent cases, but in many others as well.

Gang member witnesses or victims are also frequently reluctant to offer information, but for different reasons. They may choose not to cooperate as they prefer to dispense justice themselves. This attitude is common among gang members and serves to increase gang violence throughout the community.

THE GOAL OF PROSECUTION

Another matter, at this point, relates to the goal of the prosecution. When a violent crime involves multiple suspects, the question is frequently asked if all the suspects are prosecuted because only a few are ever brought to trial. Why would representatives of the criminal justice system seek to convict only the shooter in a gang case? The answer is simple: it is the easiest, least expensive path to a conviction. Time constraints and the heavy workloads which prosecutors carry, generally do not permit the opportunity to build a case against the rest of the suspects; but prosecutors specializing in gang cases are seeking a different approach. Almost every gang crime involving multiple suspects also involves the crime of conspiracy. With extra effort, the shooters, along with those who conspire to help them, can be convicted and sent to prison.

As difficult as the foregoing type of prosecution may prove to be, the results are far reaching. If gang members are sent to prison after playing a secondary or supportive role in an attack, they may begin to re-examine their relationship with the gang. In the past, conspirators have been able to count on being relatively safe from any heavy criminal prosecution, as long as they did not become a primary attacker. Thus, even though proving conspiracy is both difficult and time consuming, the results may be well worth the effort. Such conspiracy convictions leave the primary attacker—the shooter—isolated and stripped of support. As a result of being singled out, the attackers are more easily identified and arrested. These tactics weaken the gang's sense of solidarity, and provide a psychological blow to the myth of gang invulnerability.

Successful prosecution of criminal elements, as discussed above, can help break the continuum of gang existence by making it difficult to recruit new members. If potential members know they face arrest and imprisonment, even for being indirectly involved in gang-related violence, the number of young people wanting to put themselves in that position should drop appreciably. However it is accomplished, gang crime must be suppressed; it is an insidious, ever-present danger to the peace and safety of the innocent people of the community.

CONCLUSION

It is the hope of the authors that the reader now has a greater appreciation of the magnitude of the problem created in society by street gangs. It is also our hope that many romanticized myths associated with these gangs have been laid to rest.

The world of street gangs, as one now can see, is not the same as that depicted in films and on TV. Rather, it is one of frustration, pain, terror, and death. Disruptions of entire communities occur because of street gang activity. Citizens in many parts of our country must restrict their daily activities out of fear of these young hoodlums; while at the same time, the sustaining members of those societies, the young people who are not affiliated with the gangs, move out of their neighborhoods to safer, more conventional, areas. As law abiding citizens move from a neighborhood, a perpetual breeding ground for gangs is created and begins to spread. Thus, the integrity of community after community is eroded.

The intent of this text has not been to denigrate any segment of our society, or for that matter, the gang member himself, but rather to offer insight into the problem from a practical and empirical point of view. One should come away from reading this text with a better understanding of *barrio* or ghetto youth. To understand a gang memnber, his values, the stress that affects his personality, or his very being is not to condone his criminal activities. As an investigator or a citizen at large, the development of this understanding adds to one's ability to inquire of, and communicate with, people of different persuasions and standards.

One should remember that gang members are frequently master manipulators. Sympathy for the gang member may be a natural by-product of working with them on a daily basis. but one must not allow that empathy to cloud one's judgement of illegal activities.

The investigative techniques advanced in this text were developed over a long period of years by professional gang investigators, and have been found to work well. Enforcement officers may find that some systems and techniques advocated will require "fine tuning" to suit individual area problems or unit strengths. The authors have attempted to anticipate these eventualities and feel that no matter what the size of the department or location, these proven procedures will facilitate the daily field operations of patrol officers and investigators assigned to street gang duties.

America's Most Popular
Practical Police Books

- ☐ ea. American Law Enf. & Crim. Justice $37.95
- ☐ ea. California Criminal Law 3rd $24.95
- ☐ ea. California Criminal Procedure 3rd $31.95
- ☐ ea. California Criminal Procedure Workbook $14.95
- ☐ ea. Community Relations Concepts 3rd $31.95
- ☐ ea. Courtroom Survival $14.95
- ☐ ea. Criminal Evidence 3rd $31.95
- ☐ ea. Criminal Interrogation 3rd $19.95
- ☐ ea. Criminal Procedure $31.95
- ☐ ea. Criminal Procedure (*Case approach*) 3rd $37.95
- ☐ ea. Exploring Juvenile Justice $31.95
- ☐ ea. Fingerprint Science 2nd $19.95
- ☐ ea. Gangs on the Move $14.95
- ☐ ea. Introduction to Criminal Justice $37.95
- ☐ ea. The New Police Report Manual $14.95
- ☐ ea. Officers At Risk (*Stress Control*) $19.95
- ☐ ea. The Officer Survival Manual $19.95
- ☐ ea. PC 832 Concepts IV $21.95
- ☐ ea. Police Patrol Operations $31.95
- ☐ ea. Police Report Writing Essentials $9.95
- ☐ ea. Police Unarmed Defense Tactics $9.95
- ☐ ea. Practical Criminal Investigation 3rd $31.95
- ☐ ea. Search and Seizure Handbook 5th $17.95
- ☐ ea. Traffic Investigation and Enforcement 3rd $24.95
- ☐ ea. Understanding Street Gangs $19.95
- ☐ ea. Rutledge 5-Pak $69.95

Shipping costs: $3.00 for 1st item and $1.00 for each additional item.

COPPERHOUSE PUBLISHING COMPANY
901-5 Tahoe Blvd. Incline Village, Nevada 89451
Please enclose credit card info., check or P.O.

Credit card orders only, call:
1-800-223-4838

Nevada Residents add 7¼% Sales Tax.
Unconditionally Guaranteed!
World Wide Web http://www.copperhouse.com/copperhouse